AF371371

THE BIG BOOK OF SuperHeroes

THE BIG BOOK OF SUPERHEROES

BART KING

Illustrations by
GREG PAPROCKI

GIBBS SMITH
TO ENRICH AND INSPIRE HUMANKIND

First Edition
18 17 16 15 14   5 4 3 2

This book refers to a number of superhero-related names, words, and character designations. These references are for identification only. All designations belong to the proper holders of their trademarks. Further, this book is not an official publication for *any* superheroes (except the ones I made up!).

Also, while reading the following pages, you may decide to fly through outer space to battle the Menace of Kendor. That's great, but I can't and don't guarantee your safety as you engage in *any* of this book's activities. In fact, I expressly disclaim liability for any injury, damages, or fatalities resulting from the use of this book. So read it at your own risk.

But I'm sure you'll probably be fine, just *fine*—hey, look out for that tractor beam!

Published by
Gibbs Smith
P.O. Box 667
Layton, Utah 84041

1.800.835.4993 orders
www.gibbs-smith.com

Designed by Andrew Brozyna
Printed and bound in China

Gibbs Smith books are printed on either recycled, 100% post-consumer waste, FSC-certified papers or on paper produced from sustainable PEFC-certified forest/controlled wood source. Learn more at www.pefc.org.

Library of Congress Cataloging-in-Publication Data

King, Bart, 1962-
 The big book of superheroes / Bart King ; Illustrations by Greg Paprocki.
 — First edition.
   pages cm
 ISBN 978-1-4236-3397-6
 1. Superheroes—Humor. I. Paprocki, Greg. II. Title.
 PN6231.H44K57 2013
 741.5'352—dc23
                    2013027903

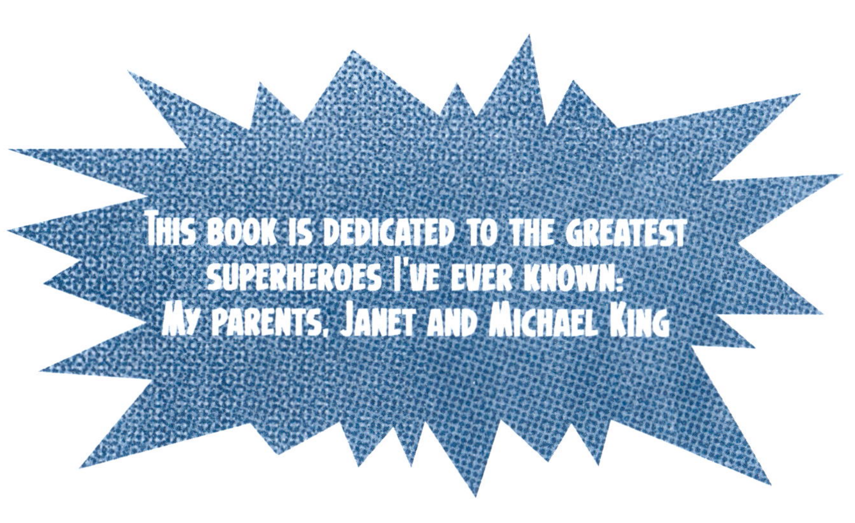
This book is dedicated to the greatest
superheroes I've ever known:
My parents, Janet and Michael King

CONTENTS

Welcome to the World of Superheroes! ... 9

Superpowers! ... 17

Acting Like a Superhero! ... 35

Becoming a Superhero! ... 57

Letting Your Parents Know! ... 73

Superhero Training! ... 81

Fighting Like a Superhero! ... 87

Zingers and Battle Cries—
     Speaking Superhero! ... 109

Rugrats—Your Most Dangerous Foe! ... 123

The Lamest—and Most Underrated—
     Superpowers! ... 133

Your Supername! ... 145

Dress Like a Superhero! ... 157

What's This "Right vs. Wrong" Stuff?! 179

Supervillains and Other Ethically
    Challenged People! 195

The Supervillain Halls of Shame and Fame! 217

Super Sidekicks! 221

Animal Superheroes! 231

Secret Lairs! 239

Superhero Teams! 249

The End Is Near! 267

Super Pop Quiz! 271

Appendix: Early Superhero History! 275

Selected Bibliography 279

Answer Key 285

Acknowledgments 287

WELCOME TO THE WORLD OF SUPERHEROES!

I have good news. By reading these words, you just became an honorary superhero. Yay!

But maybe you're wondering, "What *is* a superhero, anyway?" It's simple—a superhero is anyone who wants to fight evildoers and right wrongs. These could be small wrongs, like:

"Who used up all the toilet paper?"

Or it might be a *big* wrong, like:

"Who used up all of the toilet paper in the Secret Lair?"

Of course, you can do things your way. Instead of *fighting* evildoers, you might want to *argue* with them. (I'm pretty sure this isn't as successful, though.)

Some people say that any good-hearted outsider is a superhero. (So that could include everyone from **Luke Skywalker** to **Daffy Duck**.) But however you think of it, being a superhero can be hard. Your superpowers might spin out of control. Supervillains want to clobber you. And even nice people can grow jealous of all the attention you get.

Plus, take it from me: it's easy to get a wedgie in a superhero costume!

Superheroes got their starts in our imaginations. See, in ancient times, people told stories about gods, heroes, monsters, and villains. And many of these characters have been recycled into superheroes. For example, **Thor** was taken right out of Viking mythology. And when the **Flash** appeared, his costume was a total copy of **Hermes'** (a.k.a. Mercury), the speedy messenger of the Greek gods.

THE VERY FIRST HERO WAS A GIRL: Ancient Greek myths tell of **Hero,** a girl who tragically drowned. Hey, too bad that Hero didn't have the superpower of immortality. She'd have lived, and "Hero worship" might have been popular!

Some of our superheroes combine different mythical figures. For example, **Captain Marvel** was a popular superhero in the 1940s. His secret identity was as a boy named Billy Batson. And when Billy said "SHAZAM!" he transformed into Captain Marvel, a crime fighter with the powers of heroes and gods:

S for the wisdom of Solomon

H for the strength of Hercules

A for the stamina of Atlas

Z for the power of Zeus

A for the courage of Achilles

M for the speed of Mercury

Another hero with origins in myth is the Amazon warrior called **Wonder Woman.** She's "stronger than Hercules and swifter than Mercury," and her archenemy is Mars, the god of war. Unlike the ancient Greeks, Wonder Woman flies around in an invisible jet. (Although cool, this does raise the risk of midair collisions!)

Are there any mythological characters who are actual *superheroes*? Maybe! For instance, **Hercules** usually did the right thing. He also had superstrength and wore a special costume. (It was the impenetrable hide of the Nemean lion.)

But superheroes usually have secret identities—for example, **Batman's** secret identity is Bruce Wayne. And as a wise man once said, "Hercules was always Hercules."

IT TOOK A WHILE TO CATCH ON: People didn't actually start using the word *superhero* until the 1940s.

Their backgrounds are in myths, but almost all of today's famous superheroes got their start in comic books. One exception is the **Green Hornet,** who first appeared in a radio show back in 1936. Another one is the superhero family known as the **Incredibles:** Elastigirl, Violet, Dash, Jack-Jack, and Mr. Incredible all got their starts at the movies.

Before we go any further, I need to warn you about something: being a super-hero is awesome, but there are a few drawbacks. Here are some now!

THE FIVE MOST EMBARRASSING THINGS THAT CAN HAPPEN TO A SUPERHERO

1. Your sidekick pees his pants.

2. Just as you start battling a supervillain, your mom calls out, "I love you, honey!"

3. You come out of the bathroom with your cape stuck down the back of your underwear.

4. You fly over your school ("Hurray!"), then get motion sickness and barf on your friends ("Boo!").

5. You show up at a crime scene wearing the same costume as another superhero. (Awk-ward!)

BUT WHY BE A SUPERHERO?

What, fighting evil isn't enough for you? Fine. If you've ever thought you were meant for better things, become a superhero. If you've ever felt misunderstood by the world, become a superhero. If you've ever wanted to strike a blow for justice, *become a superhero.*

Or if you've ever just felt like wearing your underpants on the outside—**become a superhero!**

Still not enough to convince you? How about this: being a superhero will make you happier! Most people work for power, money, or fame. But experts think the happiest people are the ones whose jobs have *meaning.* And what could be more meaningful than saving the world?

And while you're thinking about that, think about this: how many superheroes actually *quit,* and go back to living normal lives?

Almost none.

And finally, just between us—remember, this is a *secret*—becoming a superhero is a great way to get *payback.* Did someone trip you in the hallway last year? Let's see how he likes dangling from a skyscraper. Or how about that kid who made faces at you on the bus? He might find himself dropped off at your zoo's Monkey Island if he's not careful!

As a certain superhero once said: "As Peter Parker, I was just a helpless, confused kid! But as **Spider-Man,** things are gonna be a lot different!"

THE MORE YOU KNOW, THE LESS YOU DON'T! During World War II, a superhero named **Miss Victory** fought the Nazis. One of her best lines was, "Heil your grandmother!"

WHY AM I THE RIGHT PERSON TO WRITE THIS BOOK?

Look, I don't want to brag, but *I'm* a superhero. In fact, I'm wearing a colorful costume while I'm typing this. Ooh, hang on—I've got trouble!

shifts in chair

Whew, that was a close call. (I told you it's easy to get a wedgie in these things.)

I admit that I'm not the greatest American superhero. But at least I'm better than lame heroes like **Fraction Man** and his sidekick, **Decimal Girl.** In fact, I'm better than *any* of . . .

THE NINE MOST UNHELPFUL SUPERHEROES!

MUD BOY: Using only water and dirt, this superhero can make . . . **mud.**

TWITTER WOMAN ruthlessly peppers her foes with one insulting tweet after another.

CALENDAR MAN: This superhero is doomed. After all, his days are numbered. (Get it? Get it?)

THE EXAGGERATOR: "The fate of this cookie--I mean, the **universe**--is at stake!"

DUMB IDEA LAD'S name pretty much explains everything about him.

SUDOKU GIRL uses her superpowers to quickly solve number puzzles and . . . **zzzzz.**

SHOELACE MAN can tie shoes very tightly and quickly. Want double knots? No problem! (His archenemy: Velcro.)

MISSILE TOE fires his toes as missiles. Then he has to awkwardly run around to collect them.

UNHELPFUL HERO HALL OF FAME: ROCK GAL!

SUPERPOWERS!

Hey, did you know you already *have* a superpower? No? Then it sounds like we need to work on your self-esteem.

So imagine you were reading this sentence six hundred years ago. *That* would've been a superpower. No, not because you traveled through time. It's because six hundred years ago, almost nobody could read!

And anytime you can do something most people can't, *that's* your superpower. For example, I can brush my teeth with either hand. Not bad, huh? And I bet *you* have unusual skills too.

So are you feeling better about yourself? Good! Now let's see about getting you *another* superpower. After all, it'll make fighting crime a lot easier. And having a superpower doesn't hurt—unless you have the power to *feel pain* better than anyone else. Then having a superpower *would* hurt. A lot!

Pop Quiz
THE SUPERPOWER KING!

This character has more superpowers than any other superhero. He is:

1. Superman

2. J'onn J'onzz, the Martian Manhunter

3. Spider-Man

(See answer below.*)

NOT VERY AMAZING FACT! You may be wondering how to pronounce a crazy Martian name like J'onn J'onzz. Well, it sounds like this: *John Jones.* (Yeah. Real crazy.)

Now keep in mind that even "good" superpowers can have drawbacks. Look at the **Thing.** Sure, he has superstrength, but it came at a cost—the Thing looks like a pile of bricks!

* Answer: **J'onn J'onzz** can read minds, become invisible, shape-shift, and create illusions. He also has X-ray vision, telekinesis, superstrength, superhearing, invulnerability, *and he can fly.* And I'm not even going to mention his vortex breath.

As Spider-Man once said: "My *powers!* What a joke! I sometimes think they've proven to be nothing but a curse!"

What was he talking about? To find out, take a look at the pros and cons of—

THE FIFTEEN MOST POPULAR SUPERPOWERS!

At this year's Comic-Con, I asked hundreds of people what superpowers they wanted most—and these were their top picks!

1. SUPERSTRENGTH

Advantage: A tight lid on the pickle jar will never stop you again!

Disadvantages: People will constantly ask you to help them move furniture. (And just *try* playing Jenga without losing.)

SUPERSTRENGTH: YOU ALREADY HAVE IT!

One of my favorite superheroes is **Asterix the Gaul.** He lived in the time of the ancient Roman Empire. Before going into battle, Asterix drinks a magic potion created by a druid named Vitamix. This gives Asterix the power to defeat the Roman soldiers. (They were meanies!)

You actually have something like Vitamix's magic potion in your body. Really! That's why news stories like this come out all the time:

> Tracy Boggins, 17, was making sandwiches when she heard a cry from the garage. There, she discovered her father being crushed beneath the family's minivan. (He was changing the van's oil when it slipped off its car jack.) The teenaged girl then grabbed the edge of the car and lifted it enough for her father to escape.

So isn't it impossible for a teenaged girl to lift a car? No! Humans can lift about *seven times* their own body weight if they have to.

Most of us never *try* using our superstrength for two reasons: First, we don't think we can lift very much weight. And second, we're afraid of injuring ourselves. But all that changes in an *emergency.* Then you don't have time to think, *"I'd lift this van, but I probably can't and I might break a nail."* You just do it!

In an emergency, your body releases a hormone called *adrenaline.* This increases your rates of blood circulation and breathing. So your muscles get an extra boost, and you're stronger! (This is sometimes called the "fight-or-flight response.")

At the same time, your body releases other things into

your bloodstream, including substances called *endorphins*. These squelch pain and make you feel good. So endorphins allow you to try harder than you normally would.

What kind of crises can give you this amazing strength? Sadly, they are very rare. So if you're squeezing out the last bit of toothpaste from a tube, see if the danger of a cavity makes you mighty!

Adrenaline and endorphins kick in when our friends or family are in peril. For instance, if you see innocent animals in a death trap like this, your hormones will spring into action!

2. SUPERBREATH

Advantage: You know when you're camping and those little bugs fly around your face and drive you crazy? Not anymore. Just blow! Now those bugs are at someone *else's* campsite.

Disadvantage: This superpower is tough on the people around you. ("Did you have garlic last night? *And* onions? Ugh!")

3. SUPERSPEED

Advantage: You could play Ping-Pong against yourself.

Disadvantages: You're going to wear out a *lot* of shoes. And no matter how fast you run, people are always going to say the same thing to you!

THE MORE YOU KNOW, THE LESS YOU DON'T! To make the Flash's comic seem real, his writers based the stories on science. So if the Flash did something amazing, there was a reason: *"The Flash can run across water because he never broke the surface tension of the liquid."* Totally believable!

4. FLYING

Advantage: This is the most eco-friendly way to travel ever. So, go green! (Wait, you're not afraid of heights, are you?)

Disadvantages: Bugs on the teeth and chapped lips aren't much fun. But flying's biggest problem is *altitude sickness.* See, if you fly more than 1.5 miles (about 8,000 feet) above sea level, you'll probably get a headache and start feeling dizzy. That's because the air is thinner up there, and there's less oxygen.

So be sure to fly at lower altitudes. In other words, don't fly in *thin* air, fly in *fat* air.

FUN FLYING FACT: Superheroes who use flying machines (like the Fantastic Four's Fantasticar and Iron Man's suit) have a problem. They must check in with the Federal Aviation Administration (FAA) every time they fly. But superheroes who fly on their own power (like Superman) don't use aircraft. That means they can take off anytime they want!

Discussion Question: Green Lantern uses a ring to fly. Would he have to check in with the FAA before takeoff?

SUPERPOWER ACTIVITY
JETPACK!

Supplies: Two empty liter bottles, duct tape, red plastic cups (example: Solo cups), red or orange crepe paper *or* spray paint.

Anyone can have the superpower of flight with a jetpack! Here's how to make your own:

continued

1. Crumple your crepe paper into small, colorful
   wads. Then stuff these into the bottles. Or paint
   the bottles silver or gold. Metallic spray paint
   looks especially good on these.

2. Screw the
   bottles' lids
   back on. Now
   cut out the
   bottom of your
   plastic cups
   and duct–tape
   them to the
   lids as shown.
   (The beauty of
   silver duct tape
   is that it looks
   space age!)
   You may want
   to tape or
   glue "flames"
   of colored crepe paper coming out the ends of
   these cups.

3. If you're ready to wear your jetpack, duct–tape
   your two bottles together. Continue to wrap
   the tape either over your shoulders or around
   your chest.

Danger: When taking off with your jetpack, remember to
keep your legs straight. (Otherwise, you'll get scorched
ankles!)

5. X-RAY VISION

Advantage: No more having to pay for expensive X-rays at the hospital.

Disadvantage: The temptation to cheat on tests would be hard to resist.

> **SUPERPOWER MARKETING:** A school cafeteria once labeled its carrots as "X-ray vision carrots." After that, carrot sales rose by 50 percent!

6. TIME TRAVEL

Advantage: You could go back in time and undo any mistakes you'd made.

Disadvantage: That would take me, like, forever.

SUPERPOWER ACTIVITY

TIME TRAVEL!

Supplies: Foil, a helmet of some kind (example: batter's helmet).

Traveling in time is one of the most excellent superpowers. To convince people you can travel in time, do the following:

1. Cover your helmet in foil. Put it on.

continued

2. Run into a crowded room of strangers (like a classroom or frozen yogurt shop) and loudly ask, "Please, someone tell me, what *year* is it?"

3. No matter what year they shout out, act utterly amazed. You might cry, "Dang it, I knew something was wrong!" and run back out of the room. Or try this line:

LONG-RANGE ACTIVITY: Do this *exact* same thing again the next day at the same place. Again, it doesn't matter what year they yell out. (Then repeat this every year for the rest of your life. What a laugh!)

7. MIND CONTROL

Advantage: Wait, how is this a superpower? I mean, I can *already* control my mind.

THE IDEA IS THAT YOU CONTROL SOMEONE ELSE'S MIND!

Disadvantage: Eventual baldness.

8. MIND READING

Advantages: Reading a criminal's mind can help you stop crime. Plus, you'll get to know what people *really* think of you!

Disadvantages: Do you have good self-esteem? Because you're going to know what people *really* think of you! Also, you know how boring it is to listen to someone else's cell phone conversation? Now imagine having to listen to stuff that dull every time you got near someone. Oh, the humanity!

9. SUPERHEALING

Advantage: No scars!

Disadvantages: Sticks and stones won't break your bones, but names *can* still hurt you. Also, this is going to happen:

10. SUPERHEARING

Advantage: You used to hate it when people whispered secrets. Not anymore!

Disadvantage: Being able to hear grass grow makes it hard to take naps. ("Could someone tell the lawn to keep it down?")

SUPERPOWER ACTIVITY
MY EARS ARE BURNING!

Supplies: Two walkie-talkies, duct tape.

Do you like to eavesdrop on other people? Me too! That's why I like to scout out spots where my archenemies (and archfriends!) hang out.

1. First, I make sure my walkie-talkies' batteries are fresh, and that they're both on the same channel.

2. Then I find a suitable hiding place for the first walkie-talkie. This might be behind, inside of, or next to something. Can't find a good spot? Try slipping it in the open pocket of a coat.

3. Next, I duct-tape the walkie-talkie's "transmit" button down. That means this walkie-talkie is now sending out a signal.

4. Finally, I go to a nearby, hidden location. If I have an earbud, I connect it to the other walkie-talkie. If not, I just turn my walkie-talkie's

continued

volume down low. Then I turn it on, go to the proper channel, and start listening!

5. After learning fabulous secrets ("Timmy likes chocolate? No way!"), I wait for the coast to be clear. When it is, I go back, retrieve the first walkie-talkie, turn it off, and celebrate my awesomeness.

11. TELEKINESIS
(MOVING THINGS WITH YOUR MIND)

Advantages: Just *think* about cleaning your room and it's done. (Plus, you can make tacos while doing Sudoku!)

Disadvantages: You have to be really, really careful what you think about.

For example, let's say your friend sneaks up behind you and yells "Boo!" And before you know what you're doing, you fire a sharp pencil right through his appendix!

Also, did you know that superheroes with telekinesis get chubby? Guess why!*

12. INVISIBILITY

SPOT THE INVISIBLE WOMAN!

Advantage: Although not as exciting as superstrength, the power of invisibility would be cool . . . but *only* if your clothes turned invisible along with the rest of you.

Disadvantage: Blindness. You "see" things as light goes into your eyeballs and reflects onto things called "receptors." But if you are *invisible,* the light will go straight *through* your receptors. That means you won't be able to see anything!

13. ELECTRICITY

Advantage: You'll be cool, because this is the most *current* superpower there is. (Get it?)

Disadvantage: I hope you like having curly hair. (*Really* curly hair.)

* The more superheroes use telekinesis, they less they exercise. After all, why bother moving when you can do everything with your mind?

SUPERPOWER ACTIVITY
THE LIGHTNING TOUCH!

Supplies: Shag carpet, a supervillain.

Electro was a supervillain who could store massive amounts of electricity in his body. He could then release this energy in the form of lightning bolts. Nice!

To imitate Electro, do the following:

1. Find some shag carpet.

2. Shuffle your feet on it without picking them up from the carpet.

3. Find a supervillain. Can't find one? Your brother will work.

4. Touch him. I know, you'd rather not. But the spark of electricity and the sound of your brother's screeches will reward you!

14. IMMORTALITY

Advantage: Not dying. (Sweet!)

Disadvantage: Not dying. (Trust me, after a few thousand years, living gets old!)

15. SUPERINTELLIGENCE

Advantage: I'd explain it to you, but you really wouldn't understand.

Disadvantage: None. Hey, finally I'll start winning some arguments!

SUPERINTELLIGENCE TEST! If you answer this question right, you're *already* a supergenius. Ready? Here goes!

Mean aliens are on their way to attack the Earth. To stop them, you build a force-field machine. Every day your machine is turned on, its force field will *double* the amount of the Earth it can protect.

It takes a total of twenty-four days for your machine to cover the entire planet with its force field. So, how long will it take for your machine to cover *half* of the planet?

Got an answer?* How'd you do? Either way, do the following activity!

SUPERPOWER ACTIVITY

ACT LIKE A GENIUS!

Supplies: A brain, preferably your own.

You can be smarter in five minutes. Ready? Just follow these two simple steps:

1. Notice stuff.

   Quick, how many steps are there in your house? I mean, you've probably walked on them thousands of times. But have you ever counted them? Probably not!

   Here's a secret. If you take the time to really

continued

* Twenty-three days. (Do the activity!)

notice the things around you, your IQ will start to rise. Seriously! It's this simple superpower that makes Sherlock Holmes such a genius.

As you notice stuff, cool things will start to happen. Look, your teacher got new glasses. (Extra credit!) Hey, you spotted an out-of-control tricycle swerving toward the playground. (Toddlers saved!) And wow, you just noticed a huge alien spaceship that's sucking up litterers with a tractor beam. (Those aliens sure are helpful!)

2. Go offline once in a while.

The best way to notice stuff is when you're offline. Even if it's just for a half hour! Trust me, this will give you a huge advantage over everyone else. That's because most people stare at smart phones, tablets, and computers all the time. That means they're noticing *less* and *less* stuff around them. (And this is making them the *opposite* of smart.)

ACTING LIKE A SUPERHERO!

Listen up! When you're in your costume, you stand for superheroes everywhere. That means you need to act like you've got superhero *style*. So for starters, always look alert and ready for action.

It's important to make a superhero-ey impression *all* the time. So let's try a couple of imaginary situations and see how you do. First, picture yourself walking down the street. Suddenly you see something on the sidewalk—a quarter. Sweet!

What should you do?

a. Ignore it. (It's just a lousy quarter!)

b. Point it out to your archenemy. ("Hey dude, there's a quarter!")

c. Bend over and pick the quarter up. (Then donate it to charity!)

d. None of the above.

The answer is **d.** Of course, you *should* get the quarter and donate it to charity. But you can't just bend over and pick it up. You have to get that coin with *style.* That means putting some "oomph" into it—including your own sound effects!

THIS IS HOW YOU PICK UP A QUARTER!

Here's another situation. Let's say that your archenemy damaged your toaster. Dang! So instead of good toast, all you get now is burnt bread. ("Looks like your toast has taken a turn to the dark side," your archenemy chuckles.)

This makes you very unhappy—and you *express* your unhappiness by:

a. Scowling.

b. Calling it a "crumb-ey situation."

c. Yelling "*NOOOOOO!*"

d. All of the above.

Again, the answer is **d.** As a superhero, you must *overreact* to every situation. Also, you should make a *bad pun* every chance you get. And finally, you need to get *physical*—like this:

Now you're getting the hang of it! But are you gasping from all that exercise? That means you're out of shape. I'll talk about training a little later (see page 81), but for now, there's one sport that all superheroes should try: *parkour* (which is derived from the French term for "obstacle course").

Parkour is all about climbing on, scampering on, and jumping over *everything* around you. This includes ledges, walls, buildings, and even furniture. So the teenagers in Paris who invented *parkour* must've really admired Spider-Man!

Practicing *parkour* will help your balance, coordination, and stealth. And it'll give you a whole new way of seeing things. The world will look like a huge playground! So, do you have any trees, fences, buildings, ledges, stairs, and walls near you? I thought so.

I'm guessing you can already do simple moves, like somersaults and triple axels. So let's take a look at . . .

VAULTING!

Imagine that you fixed your toaster. So you're in the kitchen and your toast pops up. Now what? Sure, you could just *walk* over and butter it. But think about what a super impression you'll make by *vaulting* over something instead!

1. Run at the item you want to vault. Then jump and plant a hand on the top of the object.

2. Swing your legs around as you keep moving.

3. Make a graceful landing . . . and butter your toast!

MAKE SPIDEY PROUD

Climbing is important for any superhero. That's why I'm climbing right now, even as I type this. Sure it's dangerous! And if you're that worried about me, I'll stop.

sits down on stairway

Happy? Anyway, in *parkour*, there's a style of climbing walls called "tic tac." The idea is to run *at* a wall and then bounce up and off of it.

And if you'd rather not bounce off of walls, here's another way to scale the heights:

1. Find two walls that are close enough for you to stretch across.

2. Lean against one side and prop yourself with your hands.

3. Start bringing your feet up on the opposite side.

4. Keep climbing!

5. When you're done climbing, just stop. (And please, do this before you get scared!)

Now, how do you get *down*? Oh, I'm sure you'll figure out something.

FLIPPING OFF A WALL

Let's say you were being chased by a gang of evildoers. So you sprint right *at* a wall. At the last second you jump up, do a backflip off the wall, and land *behind* the bad guys.

Meanwhile, they all smash into the bricks. That'd be awesome!

But could you ever do this? Maybe! To get started, practice jumping on a trampoline until you can do a flip. Just bounce on the trampoline to build up momentum. Then . . .

1. Try to get a good jump, straight up. Use your calf muscles and thighs and swing your arms up to get good air.

2. As you reach maximum height, tuck your legs up in front of you and grab them with both arms around your knees. Remember, you want backward momentum.

3. Arch your neck and start to throw your head back. This will help you face the direction of your backflip.

A HELPFUL "SPOTTER" CAN AID YOU IN PERFORMING THE BACKFLIP PROPERLY.

4. You'll start to go into a somersault. That's good! For a moment, your head will face the ground. Don't freak out! Keep your eyes open so that you know when you're going to land.

5. As you flip over, start to untuck your legs.

6. As you land—hopefully on your feet—be sure to bend your knees. (If you land on your head, having bent knees is less important.)

If you can't do this right away, keep trying. Because if you can't backflip on a trampoline, *don't* try flipping off a wall.

But once you *can* do a trampoline flip, find a wall that has soft grass in front of it, or at least some soft concrete. If you can only find *hard* concrete, then drag a mattress or something supersoft up against the wall.

When you're ready:

1. Run at the wall. Caution: Do *not* run *into* the wall!

2. Jump into the wall at an angle, and plant a foot on it.

3. Turn in the air and jump back to the ground.

Of course, you didn't actually backflip over and land on your feet. What, are you out of your mind? You could kill yourself trying that!

RESCUES!

You're walking down the street when you hear a scream from inside a building: *"Won't someone help me?!"*

This is cool for two reasons. First, someone needs your help. Second, you get to punch through a wall to save them! Just follow these steps:

1. Make sure you're wearing gloves and a helmet (for knuckle/head protection).

2. Warn people on the sidewalk to stand back. After all, if you knock out a load-bearing wall, everything might collapse!

3. Face the wall. Is it made of wood? Brick? Steel? It doesn't matter! Just picture a point three feet on the other side of it. Now as you punch, aim your fist at that point!

4. Go through the gaping hole you just made and save the person inside.

Optional Method: Or you could just knock on the door and see if anyone answers. (Now turn the page to see what the big emergency was!)

FLYING!

Few people realize it, but almost anyone can fly if they have the right attitude. Don't believe it? Try this!

1.   Stand with self-confidence. Make sure your feet are about under your shoulders and that your knees are slightly bent.

2.   Turn slightly to the side.

3. Raise your fists to the sky and make a determined face.

4. Fly!

What's that? It's not working? No worries. A superhero named Douglas Adams said a surefire way to fly was to just throw yourself at the ground.

Then miss.

So now I can assume you're flying. Good job! But hey—put this book down. Reading is just one of the many things you shouldn't do while flying. Sure, you could text your friends ("Guess where I am now?") or ~~pick~~ scratch your nose. But remember, you're a superhero. That means that when you're flying, you need to *look* heroic!

FUN THING TO DO ON A HOT DAY

Pop Quiz

UP, UP, AND A--WHEW!

1. In his early days, **Superman** was described as someone who could "leap tall buildings in a single bound." How high was that, exactly?

    a. 1,570 feet

    b. 98 feet

    c. 660 feet

2. The **Comet** is famous for two things. First, this superhero could fly after he injected gas into his body. The second thing the Comet is famous for is . . .

    a. leaving SBDs everywhere he streaked.

    b. being the first superhero to die on the job.

(See answers below.*)

THE SCIENCE OF FLYING

Of all the flying superheroes, scientists agree there's one whose flying technique would actually work. Which one?

   a. Angel (of the X–Men) with his giant wings.

   b. Superman's ability to rocket off the ground.

   c. Thor's method of throwing his hammer, hanging onto it, and flying off into the distance.

The correct answer is *c.* Thor really *could* fly because of

* Answers: 1. c; 2. b.

momentum––the force of a moving object. Thor's hammer, Mjolnir, is really, really heavy. So when Thor spins Mjolnir around and then throws it, the hammer has *crazy* momentum.

The important thing is for the Thunder God to hang onto his flying hammer's strap. As long as he does, this method works like a Norse charm! (But I always wondered––what would happen if Thor used a different tool, like a screwdriver?)

LANDING!

What goes up, must come down. So now it's time to talk about *landing*.

Sure, you could gently drop from the air and then just walk off. But your fans expect more from you! So try this. As you come down, drop one leg and keep your arms outstretched. Then as your other leg comes down, you can crouch and look up dramatically. This turns an ordinary landing into something with pizzazz.

If you're a nonflying superhero, you'll still be jumping down from places—and you need to know how to land on a solid surface. For short jumps, hold your body like a coiled spring. Then as you land, stay relaxed, breathe out, and don't lock your ankles or knees. Make sure to land on the balls of both of your feet.

For higher jumps, use the parachute landing fall (PLF). This is a special way to use your body like a shock absorber, so that you're less likely to get hurt.

You can practice the PLF with a short drop (like, a foot high!) onto a soft surface. The basic idea is to hit and immediately roll.

1. Look straight ahead. Tense your legs and bend your knees, holding them tightly together. Tuck your elbows against your sides. Make two fists and hold them to the sides of your face. (Yes, this looks weird.)

2. Jump, but don't scream. I know, parachutists yell "Geronimo!" as they jump. But that translates to "*One who yawns,*" and what you're doing isn't boring.

3. As you fall, keep your legs bent, and your knees and ankles together. Don't point your toes down, unless you're jumping into water.

4. As soon as you touch the ground, tuck your chin to your chest and bring your knees up. At the same time, twist your whole body to the side. Remember, your knees are still bending—the idea is not to let *one* part of your body take *all* of the impact. So you want to hit and roll!

5. As you twist to the side and fall, the outside of your calf will hit the ground, followed by your upper thigh. Keep rolling! The next thing to hit will be your butt, and as it hits, *keep rolling.* As your legs swing up into the air, the last thing to hit will be your side and back.

Congratulations! You just fell down.

Pop Quiz

SUPERHERO NUTRITION!

On Earth, Superman gets nutrition and energy from the rays of our sun. This means that he . . .

a. Goes through a lot of suntan oil.

b. Rarely goes to the bathroom.

c. Can eat, but doesn't really need to.

d. Uses his cape for a solar panel.

(See answer below.*)

SOUP-ERMAN!

BRAVERY

I think one word tells you more about being a superhero than any other.

No, not "crackers." *Bravery!* Yep, being brave proves you're superhero material. But in today's supersafe world, when do we even get a chance to *be* brave?

All the time! If you pet a ferocious, kibble-eating puppy, you're brave. If you resist peer pressure, you're brave. And if you lick the top of a battery even though it feels weird, you're *super* brave.

But one of the coolest (and silliest!) acts of courage you can do is . . .

SUPERPOWER ACTIVITY
DEFY THE HAILSTORM!

Supplies: Hail, a big plastic bowl.

Nothing is more terrifying to nonheroes than hail. You can tell this by the way they flee indoors during hailstorms.

Sure, hail pellets can sting. But the odds are very low that they'll actually injure you. And that gives you a chance to be brave!

1. When you see a hailstorm, quickly put on some rain gear.

2. Then grab a big plastic mixing bowl from the kitchen.

3. As you go outside, cover your head with the bowl, like a helmet.

continued

4. Now listen! The sound of the "magical" ice hitting your helmet is awesome. And all the nonheroes in your neighborhood will be amazed at your bravery!

Note: If there's any lightning, don't defy the hailstorm. (Lightning is also the reason you use a plastic bowl and not a metal one!)

Of course, the *best* kind of bravery is the kind that helps others. And one way for you to develop this courage might be by *playing video games.*

I know, it seems crazy. But some scientists asked, "What if kids played *superhero* video games, and their characters rescued others from danger?" So they ran an experiment! And it turns out that playing video games like this made the players more helpful in *real life.* In other words, after *pretending* to be a good superhero, kids were more likely to *act* like a good superhero.

What does that mean for you? If you don't *feel* brave, just *pretend* you are anyway. And after a while, you'll believe it.

SUPERPOWER ACTIVITY
"MISSION ACCOMPLISHED"

Supplies: Bravery, traffic.

The time will come when you save someone. Maybe you'll slap a bottle of poison out of a toddler's hand. Or maybe you'll slap a stick of lit dynamite from a miner's glove. All I know is that there will be slapping!

Or not. For example, once I saved a person's life. I was standing at a street corner and a bicyclist came up and started pedaling into the street.

"Look out!" I yelled. And the biker stopped *just* as a bus roared past us.

"I think you just saved my life!" the biker said gratefully.

Now here's what I *wish* I'd done--I wish I'd taken out my cell phone and said, "*Mission accomplished.*"

Then I'd have quickly walked away, leaving the biker to wonder what kind of superhero I was.

So keep your eyes open and be alert. That way you'll eventually be able to save someone's life--and blow their mind at the same time!

MAKING YOUR GETAWAY

Say you just completed a good deed. Great! Now old ladies want to thank you and children are trying to give you high fives. But here's some advice: *get out of there!* Trust me, you should *not* stick around. I mean, imagine Batman just caught a criminal. He's not going to give him a ride to the police station, chat with the cops, and then go to the court trial. Batman is *mysterious*. This is good for his secret identity, and it gives him more superhero cred, too. (Plus, it's illegal for witnesses to wear masks in court!)

So as you wrap up a case, write down what happened, and include any photos or other evidence you've got. Then leave that stuff with the criminal, whom I'm sure you can trust to give it to the police when they arrive!

Did you know that the **Chameleon** was the first supervillain Spider-Man ever faced? This bad guy actually dressed up *as* Spider-Man to commit crimes.

After Spider-Man helped the police catch the Chameleon, something odd happened. As the supervillain was dragged off to jail, Spider-Man ran off, crying, "Nothing turns out right . . ." *sob*

That's right, Spider-Man *bawled* after his first big adventure. How shocking! That's not how a superhero acts. Of course, superheroes have been known to behave in some pretty weird ways. Just look at—

THE SEVEN STRANGEST-ACTING SUPERHEROES!

Antennae Lad. Double-Header. Porcupine Pete. Infectious Lass. These are just a few of the heroes whose odd abilities make us scratch our heads. And here are seven of the very strangest:

1. The **Red Bee** carries a "stinger gun" equipped with knockout darts. More amazingly, this superhero keeps a small hive of special bees in his utility belt. Then when trouble shows, the Red Bee releases the bees!

2. **Hydroman** can turn his body into water. Then he hides in streams, puddles, or water pipes. And when the watery superhero needs to stop a criminal, he just drowns him! (But not to death.)

3. One weird thing about **Diaper Man** is that he's a *toddler*, not a man. Also, Diaper Man's main weapon is a bottle. He can squirt his baby formula out of it like a fire hose, or just swing the bottle as a club!

4. Billy Moon combined his excellent roller-skating skills with
martial arts to become **Skateman.** And his sidekick—a
kid named **Paco**—is a champion skateboarder. (This is
actually sort of cool, now that I think about it!)

5. There is one hero made from *five* people. See, when
quintuplet brothers named Han, Chang, Lin, Sun, and
Ho need to fight crime, they dog pile onto each other to
combine into *one* superhero: **Collective Man!**

6. **Squirrel Girl** has *squirrel* power. (Surprise!) So she has
really quick reflexes, small claws, and a tail. Also, Squirrel
Girl can communicate with squirrels. And her sidekick
is a squirrel. If that sounds like a wussy superpower, it
shouldn't—Squirrel Girl has defeated villains like Doctor
Doom!

7. The **Eye** did not have a costume or a secret identity. The
Eye did not have a job or even a *body.* The Eye was just a
giant *eye.* It *did* have superpowers, though. These included
the ability to shrink, fly, shoot power rays, and—even
though it didn't have a mouth—the power to yell.

   When a crime was committed, the Eye floated into view
   and yelled, "*I AM THE EYE!* The Eye! To whom time and
   distance are nothing—who bares a man's thoughts and
   pierces his conscience! The Eye's powers are limitless—his
   vengeance is terrible!"

   Scared? Don't be. I'm pretty sure you could keep the Eye
   away by poking it with a sharp stick.

BECOMING A SUPERHERO!

Hey, you know what? Maybe superpowers are overrated. Just look at the **Whizzer.** His superpower is being able to pee for a long time. Big deal!*

And then there's **Batman.** He's the most popular superhero ever. And do you know what Batman's superpowers are?

1. He's rich.

2. He's smart.

3. He's a really good athlete.

Not very impressive, is it? Heck, *I've* got those three superpowers.

Okay, maybe two out of three.

Fine, fine, just the *one* then. I'm a really good athlete. (You should see me play checkers!) Anyway, with or without superpowers, the life of a hero is pretty awesome. For one thing, being a good role model for children is great for your self-esteem!

* Kidding! (Actually, the Whizzer's superpower is superspeed.)

But how do you *become* a superhero? It's not always fun. For instance, the **Spectre** was a policeman who died and returned to Earth in a green and white costume. The Spectre's superpower? He was dead. (Yay.)

Then there's Fred Parrish. He got struck by lightning. Then Fred was put on a plane to get expert medical help—and the *plane* got hit by lightning.

It crashed near a secret underground lab. There, a scientist found Fred in the plane's wreckage. To save Fred's life, the scientist dosed him with radiation. And this gave Fred *superpowers.* And that's how he became the superhero called the **Blue Bolt!**

So you could follow Fred's simple steps:

GET HIT BY LIGHTNING + GET HIT BY LIGHTNING + PLANE CRASH + RADIATION
= SUPERHERO

But there's got to be an easier way. Sure, you could read this entire book. But who has that kind of time? So try one of the following methods...

BECOME AN ORPHAN

Lots of big-shot superheroes—like **Superman, Captain America,** and **Spider-Man**—are orphans. So bummer for you if you're already stuck with parents!

As for Batman, did you know that Bruce Wayne's parents got murdered in a place called Crime Alley? (I'm thinking that this was probably not the safest spot for them to hang out.)

READ A LOT

After a shipwreck, a kid named Johnny Jones got marooned on an island. For years, his only companions were the hundreds of books that washed ashore with them. So Johnny read them *all*. And that made him a genius.

After his rescue, Johnny became a superhero known as **Genius Jones.** Outfitted with a cape and crash helmet, he used his mental powers to fight evil. Or as Genius put it, he "expunges and exterminates espionage and incarcerates intriguers."

HANDICAP? SHM-ANDICAP!

Professor X is confined to a wheelchair. Tony Stark has no heart. And one of my favorite superheroes, **Daredevil,** is blind! If a disability like that doesn't slow him down, it raises the question: what *is* a handicap, anyway?

SUPERPOWER ACTIVITY
USE YOUR FOUR SENSES!

Supplies: A really good blindfold, a sidekick.

Most people rely heavily on their eyesight. But what if that were taken away? Can you develop your smell, hearing, touch, and even taste to be more "super"?

Make a blindfold out of a bandanna, handkerchief, or T-shirt. Be sure to fold it so that you can't see anything. After you are "blind," try to accomplish some simple tasks. (Oh, and be sure to walk slowly and carefully!) Some possibilities:

1. Go to the bathroom and wash your hands.

2. Get something to eat. (But don't try cooking!)

3. Draw a map of where you are.

4. Try to catch foam balls that your sidekick throws to you. (This is going to be *really* fun for your sidekick!)

Don't give up on this too quickly! Use your other senses to help you get around. It can be done--and the better you are at using *all* of your senses, the better superhero you'll be.

TAKE YOUR VITAMINS

Steve Rogers was a skinny nobody. Then he got a dose of Vita-Rays and became **Captain America.** And the **Blue Beetle** got his superpowers by drinking something called Vitamin 2X ("Good for you but death to the forces of injustice!").

Sadly, neither product is around today. So stick to chewable vitamins!

HAVE A ROTTEN CHILDHOOD

If you *do* have parents, hopefully they're totally useless. After all, parental neglect is how Professor X and **Blade** got their starts!

Oh, but are your parents *human*? If not, you might be in luck. Superheroes like **Wolverine** and **Hellboy** didn't have human parents. And look at how well *they* turned out!

* Answer: *True!* Batman was depressed about not being able to lift a six-hundred-pound boulder off of a kid. So he wanted to get stronger—but using steroids turned out to be a really bat bad idea.

GET BOMBARDED WITH COSMIC RAYS

Dr. Reed Richards was an average genius rocket scientist. Then he flew into outer space with his girlfriend (Sue Storm), a fellow scientist (Ben Grimm), and Sue's brother, Johnny. And the four of them got bombarded by cosmic rays from distant stars!

These rays changed Reed's body. Now he could stretch or squish it any way he wanted. He became **Mr. Fantastic,** the leader of the **Fantastic Four!** The cosmic rays changed the other three members of the group too, turning them into the **Invisible Girl,** the **Thing,** and the **Human Torch.**

But if all four people were hit by the *same* rays, why didn't they all get the *same* superpowers? Never mind!

FANTASTIC FACT: The further Mr. Fantastic stretches, the weaker his muscles get. So there's a limit to how far Mr. Fantastic can stretch his body: five hundred yards.

SUPERPOWER ACTIVITY
WORK ON YOUR BALANCE!

Supplies: Slackline (30–100 feet), two sidekicks, two light dumbbells.

A slackline is a lot like a tightrope. But a slackline is actually sort of flat (not round) and isn't pulled super tight.

1. Get your hands on a slackline and tie it between two decent-sized trees. Adjust it so that when you step in the middle of the slackline, it's no more than twelve inches off the ground.

2. Hold a light dumbbell or other weight in each hand. These will help you balance.

3. Have your two sidekicks help you mount the slackline in its middle.

4. Put one foot in front of the other. Keep your weight on your back leg. Hold your arms out for balance. Don't look down. Instead, look forward.

5. Can you stand? Good. Take a step forward. Still okay?

6. (For *advanced* superheroes only!) Now tie the slackline one hundred feet or so off the ground. Practice running back and forth on the slackline. Finally, have your sidekicks attack you from either end of the slackline.

IMPRESS A SUPERIOR LIFE FORM

Try to persuade a powerful alien or demigod that you are worthy. If you're lucky, it might just *give* you a fantastic superpower!

BE A HANDSOME, GENIUS MILLIONAIRE

Just ask Tony Stark or Bruce Wayne for a loan.

GROW UP ON A PLANET WITH WEAK GRAVITY

A scientist learns that his planet is doomed. *Doomed!* And everyone who lives there will die. *Die!*

To save his baby son, this scientist puts the tyke in a rocket ship and sends it into outer space. This rocket lands on a faraway planet called Earth. And there, the alien baby gets adopted by a couple named the Kents. *Kents!*

Okay, okay, I'll stop doing that. The Kents call their new child Clark, and he's superstrong. That's because Clark Kent's home planet (Krypton) had gravity fifteen times stronger than Earth's. So that makes Clark superstrong under Earth's weak gravity.

HEAVY! If Superman were back on Krypton, he'd weigh 3,300 pounds.

And *that's* a big reason why Superman can leap tall buildings in a single bound. (Which is totally showing off, when he could easily just walk around them.)

Later on, Clark also got superhearing, superbreath, heat vision, and the power to fly. Why? Hey, maybe when *you* get to a planet with weak gravity, you'll figure it out. Your best bet is Mars. If you weigh one hundred pounds on Earth, you'd only be thirty-eight pounds on Mars. (*Mars!*)

GET BITTEN BY SOMETHING MAGICAL OR RADIOACTIVE

If you're brave enough to let a creature sink its fangs into you, this might be the quickest way to superhero-dom. For example, high school student Peter Parker went to a physics lab demonstration on radiation. Naturally, he got bitten by a radio-active spider. Because of this bite, Peter gained the strength and agility of a spider.

But just think—with one slight change in the story, everything would have turned out differently.

YOU DID WHAT?! In 1973, Spider-Man accidentally killed his girlfriend, Gwen Stacy. And it really *was* an accident. See, Stan Lee (the head of Marvel Comics) was going on vacation. Before leaving, he told Spider-Man's writer to continue the story "any way you want to." And when Lee returned home, he was shocked to learn Stacy was now dead!

SPIDEY STRENGTH IS TOTALLY OVERRATED

Guess what? In real life, spiders are not very strong for their size. They are totally unlike ants, which are *really* powerful for being so small. So if you ever got "spider-strength," you might not even notice the difference!

A spider's true superpowers are its venom and its web. So Peter Parker was smart to invent a way to shoot webs from his wrists. (It was a much better idea than shooting webs out of his butt, like a real spider.)

ONE BORING CARTOON: The 1994 *Spider-Man* cartoon series had *lots* of rules that its makers had to follow. These rules included no breaking glass, no punching, no fires, no gunshots, and no harm could come to any pigeons. (Really!)

The word "dead" was also outlawed. So when a villain Spider-Man *thought* was dead shows up, the superhero says, "You? But I thought you were—" The bad guy retorts, "I'm not . . . but *you'll* soon be!"

GO HIKING!

How well do you know your neighborhood? Are there any nearby caves or mountains? If so, explore them. After all, there might be a helpful spirit, Jedi Knight, or wise old person there who can school you in the ways of superheroes.

STAND NEAR CHEMICALS DURING A LIGHTNING STORM

Police scientist Barry Allen was in a chemical storeroom watching a lightning storm outside the window when—*crack*—a bolt of lightning struck him!

The lightning shattered the chemical containers. So Barry got electrocuted and soaked with a variety of unpleasant substances. But instead of dying a quick death, Barry dusted himself off and found that he was now really, really, *really* fast. So he got himself a costume and called himself the **Flash.***

You might think this could *never* happen again. After all, lightning never strikes superheroes twice in the same place. But think again! Later on, a kid named Wally West *also* got hit by lightning in a chemical storeroom. And amazingly, Wally *also* got superspeed.

As the Flash said, it was "the most utterly unthinkable, scientifically absurd coincidence . . . in the billion-to-one category."

Yep!

> **SHAZAM!** Hey, you know the cool thing about superhero jokes? They always have a strong *punch*line.

The Flash sprints around at the speed of sound. So he should be constantly eating to keep up his energy. But luckily, the Flash can eat his food superfast too! And you wouldn't believe how fast he *poops*. (The Flash can bust a grumpy in the time it takes you to blink your eyes—and hold your nose!)

* The Flash was the first superhero to get his superpowers by accident. Thousands more would follow!

RADIATION, RADIATION, RADIATION

There are *lots* of superheroes who get their powers from radiation. For example, radiation rays from an exploding "gamma bomb" turned Bruce Banner into the **Incredible Hulk.**

But it's very dangerous stuff. Although radiation gave Matt Murdock the "radar sense" that allowed him to become **Daredevil,** it also made him go blind. So instead of radiation, try these healthy options:

1. Get "Hulk juice" by making green lemon-lime punch. Drink some. Notice anything?

2. Sit in the front row for as many 3-D films as possible. I don't know what effect those mysterious "3-D rays" will have on you, but I'm sure *something* will happen.

GET *EXECUTED?!*

Criminal mastermind Dan Watkins was sentenced to death for being very bad. But when Dan was put in the electric chair, its powerful electric currents didn't kill him. Instead, it gave him the *powers* of an electric chair!

Yes, I am shocked at how silly this is. Anyway, that's why Dan Watkins gave up his life of crime and became the superhero **Electroman.**

FIND SOMETHING COOL

You never know when you might find some spare change or a magic alien artifact. For example, Alan Scott discovered a magical green lantern at a train wreck. The next thing Alan knew, the lantern was talking to him. And then it helped him become the **Green Lantern!**

As you know, the Green Lantern is an intergalactic cop. And there are more than 7,000 *other* Green Lanterns across the galaxy. These cops make up the Green Lantern Corps. They include **Ch'p** (who looks like a chipmunk), **Galius Zed** (a giant head), and **Bzzd** (who's the size of a bee).

SUPERPOWER ACTIVITY
LOSING YOUR SUPERPOWERS!

Supplies: Any soft ball (tennis balls work fine).

Hey, just as there are many ways to *get* a superpower, there are also many ways to *lose* one. Although losing superpowers is usually tragic, let's play a game that makes it fun!

First, two superheroes stand between ten and twenty feet apart. Begin throwing the ball quickly back and forth between yourselves.

The throws should be accurate enough that you can catch the ball *without* moving your feet. If one of you drops a thrown ball (without moving your feet!), then you lose a superpower. That means the game continues . . . but the person who dropped a ball has to kneel on one knee!

Here's the order of superpower loss each time you drop a ball:

First dropped ball: One knee.

Second: Kneel on two knees.

Third: Two knees, one elbow.

Fourth: Two knees, two elbows.

Fifth: Chin!

Sixth: All superpowers have been lost. ☹

HAVE A REGULAR LABORATORY ACCIDENT

Oops! I dropped a vial.

Eek! I combined the wrong chemicals.

It turns out that saying "oops" and "eek" in a lab is a good way to get superpowers. Take Bob Benton. One moment this pharmacist was experimenting with different gasses. The next thing he knew he was transformed into the superhero named the **Black Terror.**

Later the Black Terror got a young sidekick named **Tim.** Yep, that was his whole superhero name: *Tim!* The Black Terror and Tim fought crime as the **Terror Twins.** And best of all, the Black Terror sometimes traveled to his crime scenes by *bicycle.*

Now *that's* a superhero.

DID IT WORK?

I'm almost certain that you have superpowers now. So congratulations!

But here's a warning. Naturally, you'll want to start helping the police right away. But history shows this can lead to trouble. Instead of being your partner, the police will ask lots of questions, like:

"So you have superpowers, huh? Do you also have imaginary friends?"

"Why are you wearing red underwear on the outside of your clothes?"

"Who gave you this *Big Book of Superheroes*? Do you know where we can get a copy?"

"Where are your parents? Seriously. We want to talk to them."

Hey, that reminds me. You have something serious to do—go to the next chapter!

LETTING YOUR PARENTS KNOW!

One of your greatest challenges will be telling your mom and dad about your new powers. Sure, you *could* try to keep your identity a secret from them. But don't you think your parents will get suspicious when they see your superhero costume in the laundry?

The key is to break the news gently. Try something like this:

You (serious): Mom, Dad, please sit down. I have something I need to tell you.

Mom (concerned): What is it, honey?

You: This is hard for me to say—but I'm different from the other kids.

Dad: We'll always love you for who you are. But *how* are you different?

You: Well, I don't like pizza very much. Also, I can fly.

Dad: Ha! You had me all worked up! It's fine if you don't like pizza.

Mom: Wait—*what* was that other thing?

One way to make this easier is to think of your parents as older, bossy side-kicks. And after all, it's not like the members of your family don't have their *own* superpowers.

FANTASTIC FAMILY: They bicker, they joke, they eat casserole together. Yes, the Fantastic Four are more like a *family* than a team of superheroes. (Plus, Mr. Fantastic and Invisible Girl really do act like the parents of the Thing and the Human Torch.)

Of course, it's normal for parents to worry about their children. And it's important for you to make your mom and dad feel like they're part of your super-team. So to get them on board, please hand this book to your parents right now.

THE TOP SIX TIPS FOR THE PARENTS OF A SUPERHERO!

Hello! Learning your child is a superhero can be exciting and confusing. But these rules will help your family get through it with flying colors.

1. **No superpowers on school nights.** Or, limit your child's superactivities to one hour a day.

2. **All the same household rules still apply.** After fighting crime, it's important that your child feels safe at home. So keep your family's routines the same. That means that homework still needs to be done on time. And be sure your flying hero knows that being grounded means he's not cleared for takeoff!

3. **Self-control.** With superpowered strength and speed, your child might break a lot of furniture. But remember when he was a noisy toddler? You taught him to use a quiet "indoor voice." So now it's time for a new talk about "indoor powers."

4. **Be sensitive.** Growing up can be hard for any kid. Adding in superpowers makes it extra-difficult. So if your child doesn't want to fight crime when acne is acting up, be understanding.

5. **Enjoy the benefits!**

    Father: Son, with your superstrength you can do five times as many chores around the house.

    Super Kid: What?!

6. **Your secret weapon.** Remember, you have a superpower, too. You know your child's Achilles' heel! (See page 106.)

Thank you for your attention. Now please return this book to your superpowered child.

GETTING AROUND

Hey, you just got an urgent super–text message—it looks like you have to get to a crime scene, pronto! But if you can't ride your bike at the speed of sound, you face a harsh question: "How do I get there?"

This is why your parents are so valuable. For instance, maybe your dad can drive you in the minivan. I know, that doesn't seem very super. But if you get sick of asking for rides from your parents, you can dream of getting something like the **Supermobile.**

This was a minijet that Superman built out of *Supermanium,* a metal as powerful as Superman himself. And the Supermobile had lots of cool features. For example, it was eco-friendly, because the jet was powered by Superman himself. And the jet had two giant fists, attached to metal tentacles. So that way, Superman could fly around and punch supervillains. (I *wish* I were joking.)

Of course, you might wonder why Superman needed to fly in a jet that had the *exact same powers* as him. But don't! Because right now, you need to focus on family time.

SUPERHEROES ON THE SILVER SCREEN!

Sharing time with your parents is a great way to keep your home life going smoothly. Plus, what could be more fun than **watching movies** together?

There've been gazillions of superhero movies over the years. (I've counted!) But until recently, their special effects just weren't very good. For instance, in 1949, theaters showed a series of *Batman and Robin* adventures. Since there was no budget for a Batcave, Batman and Robin kept their costumes in a file cabinet.

The Batman of 1949 was pretty ruthless, though. At one point, he threw a criminal out of a tenth-story window. Then Batman turned to Robin and said, "He's probably dead."

Yeah, probably! (BTW, all the movies below are rated PG or PG-13.)

FOUR SURPRISINGLY DECENT SUPERHERO MOVIES

4. *The Rocketeer*

3. *Sky High*

2. *Chronicle*

1. *Scott Pilgrim vs. the World*

THE FOUR GREATEST SUPERHERO TV SHOWS EVER!

4. *Heroes* (first season only)

3. *Smallville*

2. *Buffy the Vampire Slayer* (skip the first season)

1. *Batman**

THE FIVE WORST SUPERHERO MOVIES EVER!

5. Daredevil is a blind superhero. So the tagline for the *Daredevil* movie was "Justice is blind." (Gah!)

4. *Superman IV: The Quest for Peace* is so dumb it shows Superman rebuilding the Great Wall of China with his X-ray vision. (What?!)

* This show was *really* funny. At one point, Robin hangs from a rope by his teeth. After letting go, he cries out, "Holy molars!" Batman replies, "True. You owe your life to good dental hygiene." Oh, and everything in the Batcave had a big label on it. For instance, trapdoors and poles had signs reading "Trapdoor" and "Batpole." (And what a theme song: "Batman! *Nuh-nuh-nuh-nuh-nuh-nuh-nuh-nuh*, Batman!")

3. On one hand, *Catwoman* has terrible acting, awful special effects, and lines like, "Somebody killed me and I've got to find out who and why." But on the other hand, it did give star Halle Berry a new nickname: "Halle Cat."

2. I didn't even watch all of *Green Lantern.* (Hey, I felt sick halfway through!) But I did hear this line: "I, Hal Jordan, do solemnly swear to pledge allegiance . . . to a lantern that I got from a dying purple alien in a swamp."

1. How rotten was *Batman and Robin?* In one scene, Batman pulls out a credit card that reads, "Name: Batman; Expiration Date: Forever." And when *Entertainment Weekly* ranked the worst movie sequels of all time, it was the worst-rated superhero movie. *Batman and Robin* was so bad, it almost killed all future Batman films!

THE EIGHT BEST SUPERHERO MOVIES!

8. *Megamind* put an original spin on the usual superhero story line by asking, "What happens when superheroes and villains get tired of their jobs?"

7. *X-Men* and *X-Men: First Class* have great casting. (That means they found the right actors for the right roles.) Also, the films take the mutants seriously, and the special effects are good!

6. *Hellboy* has an original story and lots of humor. Plus, it gets extra credit for the scene where Hellboy has to fight horrible monsters while protecting a box of kittens.

5. *Spider-Man* (2002) captured the spirit of the web slinger with jokes and a good love story. And its sequel—*Spider-Man 2*—had all that, plus Doctor Octopus.

4. Batman films come and go every few years. The best of them is *Batman Begins,* though some people thought its sequel—*The Dark Knight*—was even better.

3. *Iron Man* has a cocky, energetic hero who's well played by Robert Downey Jr.

2. *Unbreakable* is so smart and original, it took me a while to figure out it even *was* a superhero movie.

1. *The Incredibles* is a charming, funny movie with a terrific story. Its jokes and characters make it a true superhero tale. If you don't agree that this is the best superhero movie of all time, that's perfectly okay. (But you are wrong!)

> The tagline for *The Incredibles* was, "No gut, no glory."

SUPERHERO TRAINING!

Hang on—I just got a message from a reader: "Hey, none of your ways of becoming a superhero worked for me."

What? Impossible! Listen, are you *sure* you're trying hard enough to get hit by lightning?

Okay, okay, I believe you. Sadly, it looks like you have to get your abilities the old-fashioned way. You'll have to *earn* them! Fighting crime is more dangerous for superheroes like you, because you don't actually *have* superpowers. But the good thing is that other superheroes will respect you more for this. As Superman said of Batman, "If I were an ordinary man [like him], would I show such valor?"

So it looks like we have a lot of work to do! But before starting your training, let's warm up with an easy activity.

SUPERPOWER ACTIVITY
SUPERAGILITY CHALLENGE!

Supplies: Foam balls, a yard. Optional: Stopwatch.

Want to impress your friends with your agility superpowers? Here's what you do:

1. If you have a costume, put it on.

2. Go into the yard and arm each friend with two to five foam balls. (The more friends, the fewer balls each should get.)

3. Now have them take up stations at the edge of the yard. It's up to you if you want them all on one side or spread all around the edges.

4. Now move to the middle of the yard, bow, and challenge them to try to hit you with a ball. The catch is that they can't retrieve the balls for multiple throws. As the foam balls come at you, start somersaulting, leaping, climbing, and hopping out of the way.

Okay, you're almost ready to learn about hand-to-hand combat. And foot-to-hand combat. We're even going to cover foot-to-*butt* combat. (Seriously!) And all of these are going to be useful. See, even if you know just *one* martial art—like judo—it can help you to defeat a larger opponent. But being good at *several* martial arts makes you truly mighty. Like **Batman!** He's an expert in over 120 fighting styles.*

Not only that, but Batman's a really good athlete. It's been said that if Batman entered the Olympics, he could win a gold, silver, or bronze in *any* event. Yep, the Dark Knight would get medals in sports as brutal as badminton, racewalking, and Ping-Pong.

Of course, being a natural athlete isn't enough. So Batman is constantly in training! To be a good crime-fighter, he needs good endurance. And he also has to be strong, quick, and agile. So Batman's workout schedule might look like this:

* That really *is* pretty good—heck, I only know eighty-three.

That's one tough schedule—I mean, Wednesday alone is killer. See, to learn a single **martial arts** move, a student has to practice a *lot.* Some karate masters say it takes three thousand practices to master *one* move.

But Batman knows *dozens* of different martial arts. So if he's practiced *every* move in every fighting style at least three thousand times, that's like . . . a *trillion* practice moves!

Wow. And Batman has to *keep* practicing. Because if you don't use your fighting skills, they start to weaken. It's like boiling water—if you don't keep adding heat, the water cools off right away.

There are so many different kinds of martial arts, it can be confusing to know where to begin. But here's one good choice: About three hundred years ago, a Chinese woman named Ng Mui got tired of all the robbers in her village. So Ng Mui invented a new and awesome style of kung fu. Then she taught her invention to another woman named Yim Wing-Chun. She perfected this new martial art until it became the most famous type of kung fu ever: *Wing Chun* style!

Now this will seem off topic, but trust me: Batman dresses like a giant bat to scare criminals. As he says, "Criminals are a cowardly and superstitious lot." So Batman uses that to frighten the bad guys.

And that's why *my* favorite martial art is called *t'ai chi ch'uan.* This means "supreme ultimate fist." Awesome! Just imagine the impression you can make with *that.*

BATMAN--NOT A VERY GOOD ROLE MODEL?

It turns out that Batman has killed a number of bad guys over the years. In one early story, he even knocks a bad guy into a container of acid and says, "A fitting end for his kind."

That's cold!

And that's not the only time Batman's been naughty. For example, once he shot a criminal with a machine gun and said, "Much as I hate to take human life, I'm afraid this time it's necessary."

Ha! That's such a good line you should use it the next time an evildoer annoys you.

FIGHTING LIKE A SUPERHERO!

Have you ever seen a superhero movie with no fighting?

What a rip-off! I mean, come on. Fighting is one of the coolest things about being a superhero. However, as one of the good guys or girls, you want to avoid fighting if possible. So before going into battle with a troublesome supervillain, try *talking* him out of it.

(Of course, you're secretly hoping that this won't work.)

To learn more about **superhero self-defense,** real scientists visited real school playgrounds. (Really!) There they watched little kids pretending to be superheroes. The scientists saw there were lots of "good guys" and "bad guys" fighting each other with crazy kung fu moves and imaginary weapons.

And *everyone* was making sound effects:

"Pow! Zowie! Smash!"
"Bang! Whoosh! Kapowie!"
"Snap! Crackle! Crunch!"

But amazingly, not *one* of the little kids was a *real* superhero. (What a bunch of pint-sized posers.) But still, these kids were really good at **play-fighting.** And play-fighting is awesome! Not only is it good exercise, but play-fighting also teaches you to make quick decisions. It can even get you thinking about important superhero stuff. You know, like fairness, cooperation, and who you should hit next with your foam noodle.

Sadly, there'll be times when you're play-fighting and a responsible adult comes along and breaks it up. *Sheesh!* Can't the adult see you're trying to save the world?

Adult: Hey, let's stop before someone gets hurt.

Kid 1: It's OK! Roughhousing is good exercise and helps us blow off steam.

Adult (confused): You're powered by *steam*?

Kid 2: Yes. It's our superpower.

So follow these simple rules of safe fighting. That way, adults won't meddle and you (probably) won't get hurt!

FOR BEGINNERS: THE SEVEN RULES OF SUPERHERO BATTLES!

1. Avoid play-fighting near sharp edges and breakable stuff. Instead, brawl on soft surfaces, like shag carpets, lawns, or the sands of Mars. Best of all—yoga mats or mattresses!

2. Fake punching and kicking is good. Just be careful—and avoid "accidentally" hitting above the shoulders or below the belt. Also, no choking or jumping onto your opponent.

3. You can't win all the time! That isn't fun for anyone.

4. Stop as soon as someone says "Stop."

5. If you're not hearing laughter during a battle, stop. (It should be fun!)

6. a. If you accidentally hurt someone, stop right away and apologize.

   b. If you accidentally *get* hurt, stop—and try to forgive the other person.

7. Idle threats and trash-talking are encouraged. Example: "After I hit you with my Rip Van Winkle punch, you're going to wake up in twenty years wondering what happened!"

THE MORE YOU KNOW, THE LESS YOU DON'T! You may know that one of Captain America's archenemies is named **MODOK.** But did you know his name stands for "Mental Organism Designed Only for Killing"? Wow, MODOK sounds like he'd be a lot of fun to play-fight!

SPECIAL NOTE: BATTLING SMALL OPPONENTS

Here's something I've always wondered about: since Thor is a _god_, why doesn't he just crush every foe? The Thunder God explains it this way: "[I] withhold my full might. 'Twas a gradual thing . . . [I've] mostly met human menaces. To avoid the murder of these men . . . I came to act as less than I am."

So that means Thor _holds back_ when he fights! And there's a time when you should let Thor be _your_ role model. It's when you have to battle a super-rugrat. (You know, a little kid superhero?)

It's just not cool to try too hard against little kids. I know it goes against your nature, but you should let the half-pints win. After all, nothing's more thrilling for a little superhero than beating a _big_ superhero.

As for you, nothing is better than the feeling you'll get for doing the right thing. Sure, you technically "lost." But with your good sportsmanship, you actually won!*

> ## DANGER! BATTLING SEVERAL SMALL OPPONENTS:
> Taking on a whole roomful of little rugrats presents a _big_ problem. Your instinct will be to pick one up to use as a club. Or perhaps you'll be tempted to sweep the room with your Destructo-Ray™.
>
> Don't do it! Sure, those tiny villains are asking for it. But you _still_ need to deal with them gently. You also need to be careful. Just because you don't want to hurt them doesn't mean they're not going to hurt you!

* Although, technically, you lost.

So try to employ pillows and other soft items for your defense. These will come in handy as the pint-size hordes try to overwhelm you with sheer numbers. (***Pro Tip:*** Separate one preschooler from the horde and use as a human shield.)

Finally, don't ever plead for mercy. Little kids see this as a sign of weakness, and they will only attack with twice the ferocity. (For more on dealing with rugrats, see page 123.)

MORE SPECIAL-ER NOTE: WEAPONS!

Feel free to fight using any weapon you want--so long as it's a foam noodle or pillow. I know, this seems cheap. But you can still choose from a wide variety! For instance, pillow expert Daniel H. Wilson suggests using *different* pillows for *different* fights.

Is your opponent *smaller* than you? Then grab the biggest couch cushions you can find and throw them on top of the little villain. After that, you might just "accidentally" fall on the pillows, preventing any escapes.

If you are fighting a large, aggressive villain, find a square pillow. This will give you a shield to defend yourself with. And for full-out pillow wars, arm yourself with a lumpy bedroom pillow. Just reach in the pillowcase and fold the pillow in half. Now grab the opening of the pillowcase and prepare for battle with your lumpy pillow club.

PRO TIP: Did you know that little pillows are called *throw* pillows? Enough said!

INTERMEDIATE SUPER STUNT FIGHTING!

Hollywood stuntpeople are experts at fighting without actually *hitting* anyone. How do the stuntpeople do this? They pretend! After all, a little fake violence never hurt anybody. In stunts, the rule is that the person who is *hitting* is in charge of the safety of the person *being hit.*

And now that's *your* rule, too! So if you're the hitter, don't fake-punch or fake-kick any harder than you would mind being accidentally hit yourself.

If you're getting hit, be sure to overdo your reaction. Make your fake fight seem real by reacting dramatically. That means good facial expressions and sound effects. And be sure to exaggerate your falls and crashes.

One way to start is by practicing some moves with your opponent in slow motion. And then speed it up! Here's what I mean—

SUPERPOWER ACTIVITY
SUPER-KUNG FU DISCO FIGHT!

Supplies: Three or more players; a stereo or boom box.

1. Put on some of your favorite dance music. Turn it up *loud.*

2. Now begin a slow-motion kung fu fight with the other players. Remember, this is *stunt* fighting. So you can never actually make *contact* with each other. Still, now's the time to break out any kick, chop, or body blow you want!

3. As the song continues, feel free to speed up the action. In fact, you may end up fight-dancing at superfast speed, which is also pretty funny.

Remember, the key to good stunt fighting is *exaggerating* and *overacting.* Have you ever pretended to slap someone by swinging your hand at his face and then clapping it against your other palm? (This makes the slap *sound* without the slap

continued

Another key to a good stunt fight is to *play along* with each other. For example, let's say you, the superhero, turn your back on your opponent.

"I'm a peace-loving person," you nobly say. "And you're just not worth it."

Your evil rival then plays along by sneaking up on you from behind. To make it obvious, your rival might even say, "The fool! Now I will sneak up from behind."

This gives you the chance to do something like a fake mule kick (where you kick backwards, like a mule!).

THREE GOOD STUNT FIGHTING MOVES

1. **The Knee Kick:** With your two hands, (gently!) pull your opponent's shoulders down so that you can do a fake knee kick to the head. (Your arms will block the audience's view.) This gives your rival a chance at some awesome overacting.

2. **The Hook:** A hook is a short, swinging punch that you make with the elbow bent. These are easy for your rival to pretend to get hit by, without it being obvious that there's no contact.

3. **The Head Butt:** Holding your rival's noggin, bring your head forward and pretend to smash your forehead into your opponent's. To avoid accidents, try holding your

hands over your opponent's face. Then, if you accidentally make contact, you only head-butt your hands!

SUPERPOWER ACTIVITY
HOW TO TAKE A PUNCH!

Supplies: An opponent, alertness.

If you're really careful, you'll avoid ever being hurt in a fake fight. But one day your opponent may accidentally launch a real punch. So be prepared!

1. ***Don't Tense Up!*** When a fist is headed at you, your natural reaction is to tighten up. Don't do that!

2. ***Go with the Blow.*** Try to relax and go with the punch as it's headed for you.

3. ***Exit Through the Revolving Door.*** Turn away from your attacker at a 45-degree angle. This lessens the force of the blow. And if you imagine you're pushing through a revolving door, you can keep on turning with the blow—and then come right back at your enemy!

ADVANCED SUPERHERO BATTLING!

Sure, brawling with real supervillains sounds fun. But unless your power is invincibility, you can get *hurt* doing it. The best comparison is with mixed martial arts. Did you know that two out of three MMA fights result in an injury to one or both fighters? And that's with a referee there to enforce the rules!

But supervillains fight without rules *or* refs. How dangerous! So when push comes to shove, let's be careful out there.

WHERE TO ATTACK A SUPERVILLAIN

CAPE STOMP

If your opponent is wearing a cape, he deserves everything he gets. (Didn't he pay any attention to *The Incredibles*?) So when you get a chance, close a window or door on that cape without him noticing. Then flick the villain's ear. As you run off, he will chase you—only to be yanked backwards by his stuck cape!

> **SHAZAM!** My barber totally doesn't get it. Every time I go in, he puts my cape on *backwards.*

And if you're *really* lucky, the villain will have a cape long enough for you to step on. This will allow you to do this:

INVISIBLE BUTT-KICKING

One odd thing about superhero fights is that there is often a lot of talk about butt-kicking—but no one ever actually gets kicked in the butt!

To solve this problem, try the invisible butt-kick. The key is to lull your victim into feeling safe. Do this by walking next to the supervillain (or your best friend; either way) and chatting in a friendly fashion.

Now you're ready to strike!

- As you're walking, you'll use the leg that's on the far side from your victim.
- Walk normally, but kick back slightly with that leg.
- Bring your foot up behind you . . .
- . . . and now reach over with it and kick butt!

SUPERPOWER ACTIVITY
SNEAK ATTACK!

Supplies: Your enemy's toilet.

A good way to avoid injury is not to be actually *there* when you attack your enemy. Here's what I mean:

1. Remove the back lid of your enemy's toilet tank. (Trust me!) Do you see that small water tube? It goes from the edge of the tank into the "overflow tube"--that's the open pipe sticking up in the center of the tank.

    If you're not sure what I mean, just flush the toilet. See how the water shoots out of the small water tube?

2. Now just unclip that tube from its fastener. Move it to the edge of the tank so that it's pointing at the front of the toilet.

3. Now gently lay the tank's lid on this small tube, so that it holds it where you've put it. (This may take four hands, so have your sidekick help you.)

4. Now your trap is set--as soon as the toilet is flushed, an icy jet of water will spray right on your surprised enemy!

5. When you hear your enemy scream, victory is yours! Revel in your genius from the safety of another room. (Hopefully, from behind a locked door.)

RETREAT!

I know it doesn't sound very brave. But sometimes you have to run away to fight another day. So if it's obvious you're in a battle you can't win, escape!

The problem is that as soon as you turn to run, you expose yourself to a rear attack. So first, buy yourself precious time with one of these two tactics:

- **Distraction:** Look over your foe's shoulder and say, "Mom, I'm glad you're here!" (Then run.)
- **Flurry attack:** Unleash a vicious series of blows, forcing your foe to cover up. (Then run.)

Now that you're running, your foe will probably give chase. So you need roadblocks! Slam doors behind you as you go. As you pass furniture, grab pillows and throw them in your enemy's path. If you pass explosives, grab them, set them, and throw them in your enemy's path.

But the day will come when these tactics aren't enough—and you'll feel the hot breath of your enemy at your neck. That means he's *close!*

Before he can tackle you from behind, throw *yourself* down on the ground. Just collapse into a ball! If you're lucky, your pursuer will trip over you. (And if you're *really* lucky, he'll fall down an open manhole!)

If you're being chased by someone taller than you, here's the *greatest ambush* of all time. To set it up, think about your escape route. See, you're going to taunt your enemy, and then flee with your foe hot on your heels. And there needs to be a doorway that you're going to run through. It's best if this doorway isn't at the end of a long hall. (You don't want your opponent to get a good look at it while running towards it.)

Not get some packing tape (which is clear, wide, and strong). Ha ha! Stretch the packing tape across the doorway just above where the top of your head is. Anchor it securely at both ends.

Now, go taunt your enemy. Maybe you'll say something clever ("You stink!"), or do something harmless but impish (ear flick!). You have to be annoying enough that your enemy chases you. Now, run fast and head for that doorway. You'll pass below the tape harmlessly. But your pursuer won't be so lucky!

POP QUIZ

THE HEAT OF THE BATTLE!

In one comic book adventure, Batman and Robin get attacked by a gang of criminals. So Batman called out to **Batgirl,** "Get over here! Help us! We've got a problem!" And Batgirl answered, "I have a bigger one . . ."

a. "a run in my stockings!"

b. "this kid wants my autograph!"

c. "and it has to do with guano!"

(See answer below.*)

SUPERPOWER ACTIVITY

DRAGON BALL? GEE!

Supplies: Other people with jumping ability, a camera.

Hadouken is Japanese for "surge fist." In the ancient video game *Street Fighter,* one of the special attacks is called *hadouken.* A player would thrust his palms forward, shooting a surge of "spirit energy" at his opponent.

A similar move comes from *Dragon Ball.* This is a Japanese manga series from the 1980s and '90s about a kid named Son Goku. He learns martial arts and uses power blasts similar to *hadouken.*

Anyway, to get an amusing photo of a power blast in action, do the following:

1. Find someone (or some*ones*) who can jump backwards in the air while looking like they just got hit with a blast of spirit energy.

2. Find an open area where you can create your power blast scene.

3. Position your photographer so that you and your enemies are all in the shot.

4. Get in your power blast position. This can involve slamming your fist(s) dramatically into the ground, or aiming them at your enemies.

5. Have these opponents practice leaping backwards and looking stunned.

6. Start taking pictures!

SHAZAM! What does **Green Arrow** say when **Aquaman** gets too excited? "Hold your sea horses!"

ARCHER HEROES

About eight hundred years ago, **Robin Hood** was an early "bow-and-arrows" superhero. Seriously! I mean, look at his checklist:

☑ *Fights evil.*

☑ *Has an archenemy (the Sheriff of Nottingham).*

☑ *Wears a special costume.*

☑ *Hangs out in a secret lair (Sherwood Forest).*

☑ *Has sidekicks (example: Friar Tuck).*

☐ *Can fly (hey, five out of six ain't bad!).*

Robin Hood was so cool he started the trend of archer superheroes. For instance, did you know the *second* modern superhero ever (after Superman) was named the **Arrow**? And lots of other archers followed, including **Green Arrow** and **Hawkeye**.

> **HOW "ROBIN" WAS HATCHED:** When Batman chose Dick Grayson as a sidekick, he let the kid pick his own superhero identity. And guess what archer inspired his name?

Green Arrow's original secret identity was Oliver Queen. He was out in his yacht one day when he fell overboard. Rats! So Oliver swam to a deserted island, and practiced archery until he got good. *Really* good. Then he returned to civilization and became Green Arrow. Oliver got a secret hideout called the Arrow Cave and he drove an Arrow-Car.

So, can you guess what Green Arrow *flies* in? An Arrow-Plane. (Yes, really!)

As for Hawkeye, his secret identity is Clint Barton. Hawkeye got his start in archery when he was just eight years old. That's when his parents died (of course), so he joined the circus (of *course*!). And that's where Hawkeye became an expert archer.

But both of these superheroes face problems. First, no matter how many arrows they carry, they're always going to run out! And second, shooting criminals with regular arrows leads to blood and even death. To solve the second problem, Green Arrow and Hawkeye invented lots of "trick" arrows. These have led to some funny lines, like:

"We shot off the *two-stage rocket arrow,* which released the *balloon arrow*!"

Now it's time for *you* to decide! Which archer has better trick arrows?

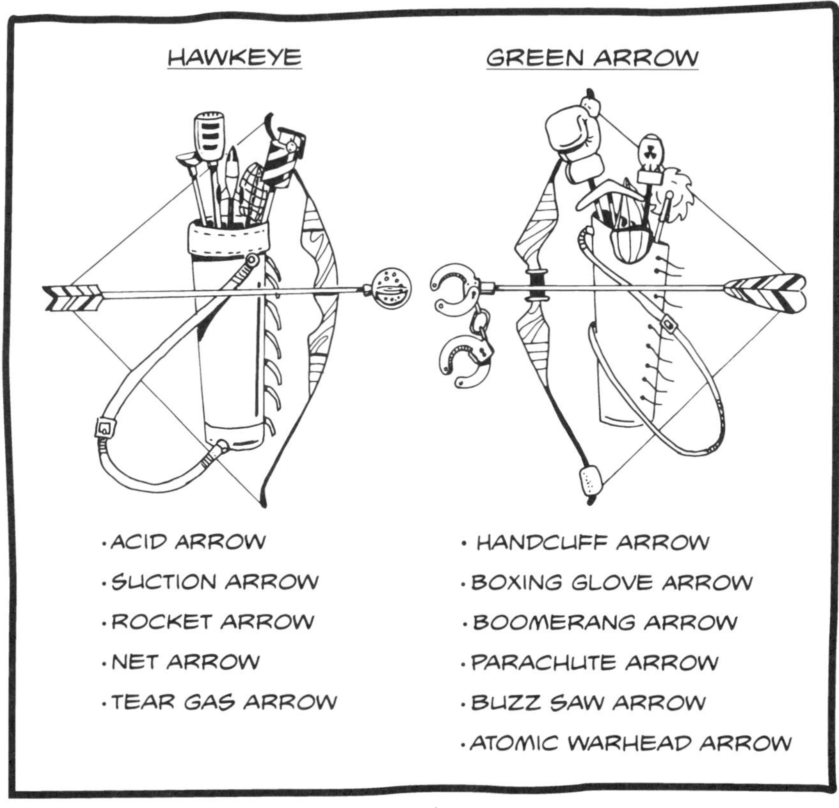

Wait, Green Arrow has *atomic warhead arrows*? The contest is over. Green Arrow wins!

YOUR ACHILLES' HEEL!

Achilles was a great hero of ancient Greece. His superpower was *invulnerability*—nothing could injure him. That's because when Achilles was a baby, his mother dipped him in magic water. (Just play along, OK?) But since she held baby Achilles by the *heel,* that was the *one* spot on his body that didn't get touched by the water.

So only Achilles' heel could be injured.

As he grew up, Achilles became a mighty warrior who killed many foes. But then a man named Paris found out about Achilles' heel. *Ha!* So Paris shot an arrow right at the hero's weak spot and—

Bam! Achilles fell down dead, like a sack of Trojan potatoes.

But here's what I don't get: why did Achilles *die* instead of just getting a *hurt heel?* ☺

As a superhero, you will *also* have a weakness, or "Achilles' heel." All superheroes do! For example, Superman can fall prey to the glowing green mineral known as kryptonite. These kryptonite chunks are the exploded bits of Superman's home planet, Krypton.

Green kryptonite weakens Superman, but there were other kinds of kryptonite too:

- **Red kryptonite:** Changes Superman's shape and personality. He might just grow a beard or change color. But on a bad day, Superman will turn into a Hula-Hoop or grow the head of a giant ant. (Seriously.)

- **Blue kryptonite:** Affects only "Bizarro" versions of Superman. (Don't ask).

- **White kryptonite:** Kills plants. (Also kills readers' attention spans.)

- **Gold kryptonite:** Eliminates Superman's superpowers for good.

So you get the idea. Achilles had a *heel.* Superman has *kryptonite.* So what do *you* have? Don't say! The important thing is not to tell anyone what your Achilles' heel is.

Not even at job interviews.

And *that's* why I will never reveal that Fig Newtons are *my* Achilles' heel. Oops—hey, forget you read that!

Your Achilles' heel could also be a *personality problem.* For example, maybe you're too proud to work with others. So even though your friends offer to help, you decide to go off to fight a giant robot by yourself.

And as a result, the giant robot squished you like a bug. Bummer! The ancient Greeks had a word for this. It was *hamartia*—the character flaw of a hero that leads to his or her downfall.

ZINGERS AND BATTLE CRIES--SPEAKING SUPERHERO!

Have you ever heard the saying, "You can talk the talk—but can you *walk* the walk?" It means you're *saying* the right things, but you have to back it up with *action.*

And action is what superheroes are all about! But when we "talk the talk," we do it a certain way. So let's make sure you're a superhero who can talk good. Or talk well. (Whatever!)

For starters, remember to use **puns** whenever possible. A pun is a play on words, like, "We've got to get Pig-Man to squeal on the other villains!" And you should also **speak dramatically.** In other words, be a ham. (Pun!) Talk in a showy, exaggerated way. And treat every situation like it's life or death. For example:

Dad: Looks like we're getting low on bananas.

You: We better *not* run out of bananas . . . or *else*!

Dad (confused): Uh . . . or else what?

You: Or else innocent people might be lost—and I'm going to *complain*!

BATTLE CRIES

Before entering a fight, superheroes often use a "**battle cry.**" These battle cries are totally useful. For example, when the Thing yells "*It's clobberin' time!*" he's doing two things:

1. He's announcing he is on schedule to clobber someone.

2. He is politely telling that person it is now time to get clobbered.

A good battle cry will *scare* your opponent and *inspire* your bravery. It's like you become your own cheerleader! And cheerleaders can be totally helpful—or why else would so many sports teams have them?

Sadly, superhero teams don't have cheerleaders. That's why the **Avengers** all have to yell "*Avengers assemble!*" themselves before going into battle. Sure, it's not the greatest cheer. But it's much more impressive than "*Avengers, gather your chairs around!*" or "*Avengers join hands!*"

WHY THERE ARE NO SUPERHERO CHEERLEADERS

Of course, even the best battle cry is useless if you don't *yell* it. (This is why you never hear about "battle whispers.") And make sure your battle cry is catchy and inspiring. That cry has got to get you fired up for the fight ahead. So take it from me—yelling "*Don't break my glasses!*" isn't helpful.

THESE BATTLE CRIES ARE TOUGH TO BEAT: The **Tick** goes into battle yelling "*Spoon!*" And the **Teenage Mutant Ninja Turtles** enter fights with a loud "*Cowabunga!*"

"TO ME, MY X-MEN!"

The **X-Men** are so popular, even their sound effects and catchphrases are popular. Here are some of them--match the sound effects and catchphrases in the first column with their meanings in the second column. (See answers below.*)

1. *mutie*
2. *snikt!*
3. *Elf*
4. *fastball special*
5. *Bub*
6. *bamf!*

a. The sound of **Nightcrawler** teleporting

b. When a strong superhero throws another character at something

c. Insult given to mutants by "normal" people

d. Wolverine calls everyone this

e. Nightcrawler's nickname (he has pointy ears)

f. The sound Wolverine makes extending his claws

* Answers: 1. c; 2. f; 3. e; 4. b; 5. d; 6. a.

SUPER TRASH-TALKING

Have you ever noticed that right in the middle of a crazy situation, a superhero might zing his opponent with a funny **one-liner**? Like when Spider-Man first met **Kingpin** and he noticed how fat he was. So the Webhead said, "Will I be fighting any of your henchmen, or did you already eat them?"

Good one! And if Spider-Man uses one-liners, you should, too. (It's super peer pressure.) But it can be hard to come up with a witty remark while avoiding a death ray. So memorize some zingers beforehand.

BAD ZINGERS

"Time out!"

"This ends *here*! Or over *there*. Either way."

"I'm telling Mom what you did!"

SO-SO ZINGERS

"Your powers are growing weaker, scoundrel!"

"Surrender now, and I might let you live."

"You only delay my inevitable victory!"

GOOD ZINGERS

"Taste the knuckle sandwich of justice!"

"Show me your organ donor card, so I know where *not* to punch you."

"I don't like your ugly face—but luckily, I have two fists to change it with!"

MOTTOS!

A **motto** is a saying that is linked to a superhero's personality. And it can be really short. For example, the **Punisher's** motto is "The guilty will be punished." That's it!

But even with just a few words, a good motto can explain who a superhero is and what he or she stands for. So it's sort of like a business card. In fact, after knocking out a criminal, the superhero named the **Clock** would leave an *actual* business card at the scene of the crime with his motto: "The Clock has struck."

Some superheroes are more long-winded. The worst is Green Lantern. When he recharges his ring, it takes him forever to recite his motto:

"In brightest day, in darkest night,
No evil shall escape my sight.
Let those who worship evil's might
Beware my power—Green Lantern's light!"

SLOGAN MAN!

"Up in the sky--look! It's a giant bird! It's a plane! It's *Superman!*"

That's how Superman's radio show began back in the 1940s. And it had loads of catchy slogans and mottos. Other classics included "Up, up, and *awaaaay!*" and "This looks like a job for *Superman!*"

By the 1950s, Superman had his own TV show. It started like this: "Faster than a speeding bullet! More powerful than a locomotive! Able to leap tall buildings in a single bound! Yes, it's Superman . . . who, disguised as Clark Kent . . . fights a never-ending battle for truth, justice, and the American way!"

A snappy motto will give you "street cred" (or, if you can fly, "air cred"). So don't settle for lame ones like these:

I think I can! (But if I can't, no big deal.)

This looks like a job for—someone who's not me.

Time for peanut butter!

I'm sort of busy right now.

Ooh, I think I just hit my funny bone!

I don't want any trouble.

If my costume gets stained, someone's gonna get it!

This will sound weird, but sometimes a good motto doesn't even have to make sense. For example, the **Cape's** motto is awesome: "One man, one fight, one right."

What does that *mean*? Who cares? It sounds cool!

Remember, you have to live with your motto for a long time. So don't put too much pressure on yourself! Take the **Black Hood.** His motto was, "Neither threats nor bribes nor bullets nor death itself shall keep me from fulfilling my sacred vow . . . to erase crime from the face of the earth!"

Sheesh. Exaggerate much? How about a promise that's easier to keep: "Neither name-calling nor water balloons will stop me from keeping my promise to put on clean socks at least twice a week."

I know this seems like a lot to remember. So if creating the perfect motto or slogan is too much stress, don't worry. Just dust off an old classic and make it work for you.

FANTASTIC DEALS! Do you know how the Fantastic Four are different from other superheroes? They run their own FF gift shop! In it, the heroes sell souvenirs with their names, faces, and logos.

Pop Quiz

MOTTO MATCHING!

Iron Man's motto is "I am Iron Man." Duh! See if you can match these superheroes with their slightly less obvious mottos (see answers below*):

1. *Superman*	a. "Sworn to protect a world that hates and fears them."
2. *The Human Torch*	b. "Imperius Rex!"
3. *Red Sonja*	c. "By the goddess!"
4. *Sub-Mariner*	d. "Flame on!"
5. *Wolverine*	e. "Whatever the battleground . . . whatever the foe . . . I shall never falter!"
6. *Storm*	f. "I'm the best in the world at what I do, Bub, and what I do ain't very nice."
7. *The Hangman*	g. "My bark is worse than my bite."
8. *The X-Men*	h. "Beware criminals, you can not outrun your conscience . . . nor escape the gallows!"
9. *Tree Girl*	i. "He fights for truth, justice, and the American way."

* Answers: 1. i; 2. d; 3. e; 4. b; 5. f; 6. c; 7. h; 8. a; 9. g.

EXPRESSIONS OF DISMAY

As a superhero, you'll see many tragic scenes of destruction. This may be a city that a supervillain has totally destroyed (*"Good grief!"*) or perhaps it will be your sister's messy room. (*"Noooo!"*)

That's when you must express the pain in your soul with a good **expression of dismay.** For example, Wonder Woman will cry out, *"Suffering Sappho!"* Thor might let loose with an *"Odin's beard!"* The **Sub-Mariner** could exclaim, *"Great pickled penguins!"* And Robin's been known to shout, *"Holy Long John Silver!"*

Meh. You can do better than those. And I have a suggestion!

THE BEST EXPRESSION OF DISMAY EVER

In 1937, a giant airship named the *Hindenburg* caught fire. As the *Hindenburg* burned and fell to earth, a radio reporter broadcast his horror:

> *"This is the worst of the worst catastrophes in the world . . . it's a terrific crash, ladies and gentlemen. It's smoke, and it's flames. . . . Oh, the humanity!"*

Since then, "Oh, the humanity!" has become famous. And strangely, it's even taken on a funny meaning. "Oh, the humanity!" has been used many times in movies, television, and even text messages. Yet somehow it never gets old! For instance, a soldier in the comic book titled *Doom* uses it:

> *"Even if I personally stop this alien invasion, what kind of planet will we be leaving to our children? And our children's children. . . . Oh, the humanity! My big gun is out of bullets!"*

As you can see, you should use this phrase as much as possible. Let's say you're at a birthday party. Every time a kid pops a balloon, shout, "*Oh, the humanity!*"

And it's also easy to make puns with this saying. (Remember,

superheroes *love* puns.) For instance, if Aquaman got hit by a harpoon, you'd cry out, "*Oh, the Aquamanity!*"

Pop Quiz

CANCELLED!

This superhero team was introduced in the 1960s. But it was such a dud, their comic was soon cancelled. These total losers were . . .

a. The X-Men

b. Alpha Flight

c. The Justice League of America

(See answer below.*)

THE GREATEST SUPERHERO SAYING (WASN'T SAID BY A SUPERHERO)

Superheroes have given lots of great speeches over the years. Yet the most famous words about being a superhero came from an old guy named **Uncle Ben.**

And he was no superhero! Uncle Ben was Peter Parker's uncle. And after learning that his nephew was Spider-Man, Uncle Ben said, "With great power there must also come—great responsibility." (The 2002 *Spider-Man* movie shortened it to, "With great power comes great responsibility.")

And the cool thing about this saying is that you can put almost *any* words after one of the "greats" and it gets even better! For example: *"With great power comes great underpants."* Or: *"With great underpants comes great responsibility."* Hey, are you a funny superhero? Try "With great power comes great hilarity."

SUPERHERO QUOTES!

Thor: Loki is beyond reason, but he's of Asgard and he's my brother.

Black Widow: He killed eighty people in two days.

Thor: He's adopted.

--From The Avengers

Superheroes may fight for good, but that doesn't stop them from saying goofy things—like these!

"I couldn't think of one clever way to stop this guy, so I just trusted to mindless violence."—*Robotman*

"Disco music—ruining my concentration!"—*Alley-Kat-Abra*

"To think that a lost land of dinosaurs could exist in the Rockies is just astonishing!"—*Wonder Woman*

"You wouldn't happen to be the Home Ec teacher, would you?" —*Spider-Man, speaking to the Green Goblin after the supervillain attacked his high school*

"The reason I was unable to detect his brainwaves is . . . his brains are missing!"—*Moondragon*

"What? A fist coming through the wall! Sure hope that whatever is attached to it is friendly."—*Angel, of the X-Men*

"If a man chooses to do something evil . . . it becomes my sacred duty to bash him to a pulp."—*Crime Crusher*

"Tough, but that's what happens to nasty villains who play with disintegrator rays."—*J'onn J'onzz*

"You don't have to be human to want to get down and boogie."—*Automan*

"If I don't get to get out and take a shower soon, I'm going to start screaming."
—*Pepper Potts (wearing the "Iron Woman" suit Tony Stark made for her)*

"I'm not afraid to die, but I can't be killed now, when the American people need me!"—*the Black Marvel*

"My common sense is tingling."—*Deadpool*

"The only reward I seek is the eventual extinction of all crime and suffering."
—*the Clown*

"Unhand those ears!"—*Color Kid*

"The contra-magnetic field of my wonder belt will repel your blade! Plus, I can sock your ugly jaw—like this!"—*the Human Meteor*

"I am normal. It's the rest of the world that's weird." —*Impulse*

RUGRATS--YOUR MOST DANGEROUS FOE!

Since you're a superhero, adults will sometimes hire you to fight evil.

But *they'll* call it "babysitting."

What a challenge! Watching rugrats can be dangerous work, even for someone like you. And it gets especially crazy when those rugrats *also* have superpowers. I mean, Little Timmy may be able to breathe underwater—but he can't even tie his shoes!

In order to avoid disaster, you're going to want to have some good superhero activities for Junior to do. And here are some now!

SUPERTOT ACTIVITY
WHO WANTS TO FLY?

Supplies: Mattress or futon.

1. Place the mattress (or futon) on the floor, and make sure there are no sharp, hard objects anywhere near it.

2. Tell your supertot to take off his shoes.

3. Lie down on the floor next to the mattress, with your toes touching it. Scoot in so that your knees are bent.

4. Have the supertot put his hands on your knees and his feet in your hands.

5. Make sure the little fellow is ready. When he is, give him some kind of a countdown. (I recommend "Up, up, and *away!*")

6. Launch the supertot onto the mattress. Remember, you have superstrength, so be careful not to throw him too far--or he'll miss the mattress!

SUPERTOT ACTIVITY
GOING INTO ORBIT

Supplies: Sturdy bed.

1. Go around the bed and make sure there aren't any dangerous objects nearby.

2. If yoga mats or foam pads are around, lay them down near the "landing area." If not, just use some clothes or stuffed animals.

3. Look up. Is the ceiling ten feet up or higher? (For comparison, ten feet is how high a basketball hoop is.)

4. Do you weigh over one hundred pounds? If so, you're just going to *tell* your supertot how to do this. But if you're a lightweight, you can do the activity too.

5. Have the supertot take off her shoes and get on the bed. She gets *three* jumps. She should bounce *once* in the middle of the bed, *once* closer to the edge, and *finally* right on the bed's edge.

6. For that last jump, the supertot should drop her butt down so that it really does land on the edge of the bed. At the same time, she pushes with her hands as she bounces up. This will give her better liftoff for going into orbit!

continued

* * *

HANDLING SUPERTANTRUMS

When little kids have temper tantrums, it can be sort of funny. Look, Junior is shouting and throwing marshmallows!

But when *super*-Junior is shouting and throwing *minivans,* it's not funny anymore. That's when a babysitter has to get tough! So your role model can be **Granny Goodness.** She was hired by the villain **Darkseid** to run his day-care center on Apokolips. And Granny Goodness only has two babysitting methods: *brainwashing* and *torture.*

Hmm, but maybe that's a little harsh. There must be other ways to prevent supertantrums. For one thing, try entertaining that little ~~monster~~ child. For example, impress your tot with your ability to walk down invisible steps!

Just station yourself behind a couch or other waist-high barrier. Start at one end, and take little steps forward. Exaggerate the swing of your arms as you go. And with each step, crouch a little more until you're waving goodbye.

SADLY, ONCE YOU'VE GONE DOWN THOSE
STAIRS, YOU'RE TRAPPED FOREVER!

SUPERTOT ACTIVITY

SUPERBREATH!

Supplies: Balloons.

Here's one surefire way to distract your child from spazzing out--bribery! Say, "If you're good, I can teach you how to hold your breath for ten minutes." That'll get any supertot's attention.

1. Have the child breathe deeply, in and out, for thirty seconds.

2. Hand her a balloon.

continued

> 3. Tell her to blow it up.
>
> 4. When the balloon is full, tie it off for her.
>
> 5. Hand the balloon back to the supertot. Now tell
>   her to hold the balloon for ten minutes. (See,
>   it's full of air from her lungs, so it's not like you
>   actually *lied.*)
>
> 6. Enjoy ten minutes of peace and quiet.

To learn more about preventing temper tantrums, let's study a superhero with a slight anger problem—the **Incredible Hulk.**

His secret identity is a shy scientist who only weighs 128 pounds named Bruce Banner. But when Banner gets mad, he's transformed into an eight-and-a-half-foot-tall green behemoth who screams, *"Hulk smash!"* What a big baby.

If you can avoid situations that'd make Hulk "smash," you also know how to prevent kiddy temper tantrums. And luckily, someone actually listed all the things that make Bruce Banner transform into the Hulk. These include:

- **Having a bad dream.** ("Mommy? Hulk smash!")

- **Dealing with a pesky operator in a phone booth.** ("Hulk not *have* twenty-five cents!")

- **Having wet towels snapped at him.** ("Owie!")

- **Being run through a car wash.** ("Suds? Hulk smash!")

- **Kicking over a beehive and then being surprised the bees are angry.** ("Sticky? Smash!")

- **Being stuck in rush-hour traffic.** ("Hulk late for dentist appointment!")

- **Having his pants catch on fire.** ("Liar! Liar! Hulk smash!")

- **Being pushed out of a plane at thirty thousand feet.** ("Hulk not get pretzels yet!")

- **Getting locked in a cage with an angry gorilla.** ("Hulk not get banana yet!")

- **Being thrown into a cactus bed.** ("Ouch! Ooh! Aah! Hulk in pain!")

THE INCREDIBLE SULK

Hey, were you successful at stopping any temper tantrums? If so, be sure to reward your supertot. Maybe you and the little sprog can work on this art project together!

SUPERTOT ACTIVITY
SUPERPOWERED SIDEWALK!

Supplies: Sunlight, sidewalk chalk, sidewalk, digital camera, supertot.

Take your supplies outside and stand so the sidewalk stretches to either side of you.

1. Working together, use the chalk to draw a big, simple city scene. Be sure to sketch in tall buildings, trees, and maybe even a cloud or two.

2. Leave an open section of air in the center of your mural. There you're going to draw a big cape flowing in the wind. Don't worry, we'll attach a superhero to it in just a moment.

3. When you're done, the scene you've drawn should take you four or five strides to get from one side to another. Now have your supertot lie down on his side on the sidewalk next to where you've drawn the cape. The idea is that, from above, it looks like he's wearing the cape.

4. Have the supertot get in his best "flying pose," with hands stretched out in front of him and a brave expression.

5. Once everything's perfect, stand above him with the camera and take a picture! (Oh, and if you're too short, you may have to set up a chair to get the proper "flying" shot.)

YOUR GREATEST CHALLENGE!

Here's the worst problem you might face. And it's so bad, it's enough to make Wolverine weep.

Let's say that you notice Junior is a little bit stinky. Okay, he's a *lot* bit stinky. That can mean only one thing: he needs his diapers changed, and pronto!

But be careful—superpowered babies are known for their *radioactive poop.* So before you open the gates of stinkiness, you need to be properly protected. For starters, I suggest a "hazmat" suit. ("Hazmat" is short for hazardous materials.) Then get a pair of tongs so that you can safely remove the soiled diaper from the child. But beware—these radioactive substances pose harsh dangers.

You, gazing in terror at the baby's toxic waste: *Never have I met a more deadly villain!*

SPEAKING OF EMISSIONS: There's actually a superhero named **Hazmat.** Since she gives off deadly radiation, Hazmat wears a hazmat suit to protect others.

THE LAMEST-- AND MOST UNDERRATED-- SUPERPOWERS!

Every person looks at superpowers in their own way. For example, here's how a little kid defined a famous hero's superpowers:

"The Hulk is a big green monster and when he needs to get things done, he turns into a scientist."

Ha! The little sprite got it backwards! (Or did he? ☺)

Since you're a hero, you probably have supersenses. But "normal" people? Not so much. The poor things have bad eyesight, lousy hearing, and they can't smell very well either. That means they can be easily confused—and this can be hilarious! Here, let me show you what I mean.

LAME SUPERPOWER ACTIVITY

GIVING SOMEONE IMAGINARY PAIN!

Supplies: A friend, and a hot dog or long cookie (like biscotti or a Twix).

Be very calm. Explain to your friend that you'd like to try a cool science experiment. (Or come up with some other lie!)

1. Have your friend sit at a kitchen table with both fists' knuckles resting against the edge of the table.

2. Have your friend extend the right index finger forward.

3. Place the hot dog or cookie where the left index finger would be if it were extended.

4. Say that you are going to gently tap both the index finger *and* the cookie from front to back. As you tap, calmly ask if your friend feels his or her index finger being touched. (The answer will, of course, be "Yes.")

   Then ask if he or she can feel you touching the cookie. (The answer will be "What? Are you insane?")

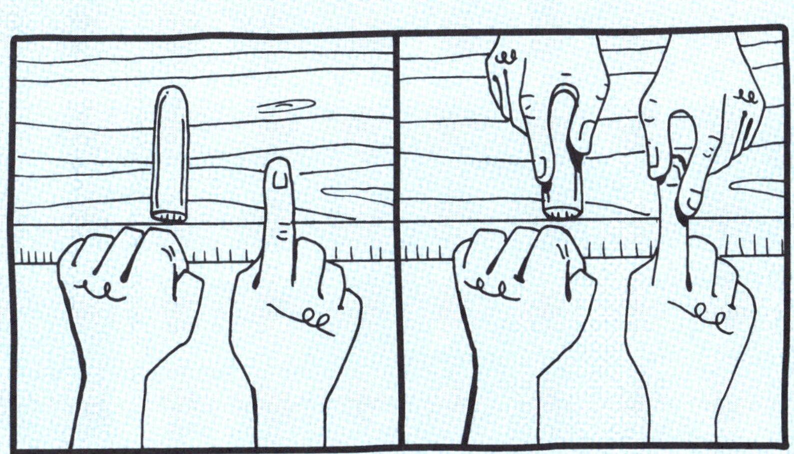

5. When you're sure your friend is relaxed, take your fist and swiftly *smash* the hot dog or cookie. Amazingly, your friend will cry out in pain! But it's *imaginary* pain that you created by being so awesome.

Optional: For extra drama, use a metal ladle or hammer to smash the hot dog or cookie. (And be careful to avoid the real finger!)

Hey, I told you that was a lame superpower! Speaking of which, I have a friend with a weird ability. He randomly *sticks* to things. This *is* annoying (*"Can someone get me down from this ladder?"*), but at least he got a cool name: **Adhesive Lad!**

And then there's **Kid Psycho.** He can move things with his mind. (This is called "psychokinesis.") At first, that sounds cool. The problem is that every time Kid Psycho uses this superpower, his life gets shortened by one year.

What a rip-off! So in honor of the short-lived Kid Psycho, here are . . .

THE TEN LAMEST SUPERPOWERS!

1. **Magnetism:** I don't care what **Magneto** says, this power
   has *many* drawbacks. But at least toddlers would like you!

2. **Being Able to Turn to Stone:** The character named
   Stone Boy can turn into a rock. And when he's a rock,
   Stone Boy can't move. Wow! There's got to be lots of ways
   this superpower is useful.

   thinking

   Let me get back to you on that.

3. **Two Words**—*Poop Vision.*

4. **Being Able to Change an Object's Color:** The hero known as **Color Kid** has the superability to alter the color of *anything.* So Color Kid can take an orange from the fruit bowl and turn it blue. Imagine that—you could eat a *blue* orange!

   Yippee.

5. **Having Supersmell:** This superpower would make it easy to track down criminals. But wait—anything that *stinks* would be your kryptonite!

6. **I Have a Feeling This Is Silly:** Greer Grant was just an average housewife. But after some experiments, Greer became the hero known as the **Cat.** And her superpowers included having really, really good "women's intuition."

7. **Seeing Just a Little Bit Into the Future:** The character known as **Ticktock** could only see sixty seconds into the future. I'm guessing this would not be useful.

   Ticktock (putting bread in the toaster): Soon, I shall have . . . *toast!*

8. **Being Scratch Resistant and Dishwasher Safe:** Raise your hand if you want this superpower!

   Yeah, that's what I thought.

9. **The Power to Scream So Loudly, Criminals Faint:** This was the power of a superhero called **Banshee.** Talk about annoying! Even Banshee's superhero friends didn't like to fight crime with him.

10. This.

But for every superpower that *seems* good but is actually lame, there's another power that *seems* lame but is actually awesome. And here's one now!

Underrated Superpower Activity

THE SUPERPOWER OF . . . OH, JUST READ THIS!

Supplies: Dog food, toilet.

1. Some dry dog foods are made in the shapes of things like stars and dog bones. Get some of this dog food!

2. Take a handful of the dog food and throw it in the toilet. (Just trust me!)

3. The dry dog food will soak up water and start bloating and growing. So the pieces of kibble will turn into *big* brown stars and dog bones!

4. That's when you're ready to call in a parent or other easily impressed adult.

   Adult (pointing in horror at the toilet): How did you do *that?*

   You: It's a superpower!

THE TEN MOST UNDERRATED SUPERPOWERS!

1. **The Power to Turn "Creamy" Peanut Butter into "Chunky":** And the people rejoiced!

2. **Being Able to Wear a Fishbowl on Your Head:** This could be handy for some situation I can't think of right now.

3. **The Ability to Have Zero Unread E-mail Messages in Your In-Box:** Never mind. This could never happen.

4. **Being Able to Embarrass Your Friends:** How awesome would this be? Imagine a car pulling up in front of a crowded school. As your best friend gets out, you shoot "embarrassment beams" at his mom, who's behind the wheel.

   Mom: I love you, honey! And don't forget, you have ballet lessons after school today!

5. **Being Able to Understand Foreign Languages:** When President Barack Obama was asked what superpower he wanted, this is the one he chose.

6. **The Ability to Walk on Your Hands:** All you have to do is bend over, stick your fingers under the toes of your shoes, and start walking around. You'll look so cool, I'm sure everyone will be impressed!

7. **Blowing a Gum Nose Bubble:** Just chew some bubblegum for a while. Once it's soft, you can stretch it out over your nose until you have a tight seal. Hold the gum's edges down and blow.

8. **The Ability to Crush Internet Trolls:** Can I have this one? Oh please, oh please?

9. **Having Farts That Never Stink:** And the people *really* rejoiced!

10. **Being Sort of Invulnerable:** Studies show that cussing helps people deal with pain. In other words, "bad" words can make the hurting go bye-bye! So how cool would it be if you were invulnerable because of your superpowered swearing?

DEATH FROM THE SKY!

Say you were standing on the sidewalk at the bottom of the Empire State Building. Looking up, you see something small falling. Someone threw a dime off the top of the skyscraper. And it's coming right at you. Then the coin hits you--*BAM*--right in the head!

So, would you be dead? After all, that dime hurtled down for hundreds and hundreds of feet. Nope. It turns out that the fastest speed (or "terminal velocity") of a falling dime is about thirty miles per hour. So that's enough to *hurt* you, but not enough to make you cry. Plus, look on the bright side--you just made ten cents!

UNDERRATED SUPERPOWER ACTIVITY
SUNDOWNER!

Supplies: The sun, your hand.

Knowing when it's going to get dark is very useful. For instance, it can help you get home by dinnertime, and also avoid vampires.

So if it's afternoon and you're wondering how much daylight you have left, just find the sun. *But don't look at it!* Instead, do this:

1. Hold your right hand away from you, with the fingers pointing to the left. They should be straight and together. Now lift your hand up, with the palm facing you and your fingers straight out.

2. Hold the top of your top finger just *underneath* the sun. *Don't look at the sun.*

3. Each finger width between the *bottom* of the sun and the horizon counts for fifteen minutes of sunlight. So if you have two fingers above the horizon, it's thirty minutes till nightfall.

If you have more than one hand's worth of space between the bottom of the sun and the horizon (four fingers = two hours), just hold your left hand beneath your right. (That gives you another four fingers to calculate with!)

THE MOST UNDERRATED SUPERPOWER OF ALL!

"You don't have to make a speech, big shot! We understand! We've gotta use that power to help mankind, right?"

—*The Thing*

As a superhero, you want to help others. The cool thing is that *you* get to decide who those "others" are! So if you're an animal lover, you could walk your neighbor's dog, volunteer at a local animal shelter, or donate money to nonprofits like the Humane Society.

If your heart goes out to kids in the hospital, maybe you can donate your hair to a group like Locks of Love or Wigs for Kids. They make wigs for children who've lost their hair because of medical problems. Or you could also just *go* to the local children's hospital and use your superpowers to brighten someone's day!

The point is that when you *make the world a better place,* you're using the most underrated superpower of all.

I know, it sounds cheesy. But guess what? It's also *true!*

YOUR SUPERNAME!

Wow, I almost forgot something important. What are you going to *call* yourself? After all, having the right name can really help—or hurt—your super-hero career.

How should you pick a name? The obvious way is to combine your super-power with your gender; for example, **Stinky Boy.** But you can see the problem with that name. That's right, the "Boy"!

Names that indicate a person's age, like Lightning Lad, Bouncing Boy, or Saturn Girl, are just silly. In a few years, Bouncing Boy will grow up. What then? Is he Bouncing *Young Adult?* What about down the line? Bouncing *Geezer?*

Hmm. Actually, I kind of like the sound of that!

Or you could take the path blazed by the Human Torch. For a name like his, you just take the word *human* and put it in front of your superpower. Since "Human Torch" is taken, you might choose the **Human Flashlight, Human Candle,** or **Human Nightlight.** (That'll impress the criminals!)

* Answer: b.

FOUR NAMES THAT ARE SO BAD, THEY'RE GREAT!

Back in the 1990s, there was a supervillain named **Dreadlox.** Know why she had that name?

She had dreadlocks.

Another personal favorite is the tiny superhero named **Minimidget.** How small was he? Let's just say that he was small--even for a midget.

And there's another superhero who's famous for his negative attitude: **NoMan.**

And finally there's **Forearm.** He's a guy with *four arms.* So his name is Forearm. Get it? He has *four arms.*

Using this logic, my superhero name should be **Facepalm.** (Because that's what I'm doing right now!)

The X-Men have one of the most popular superhero names ever. This led to imitation names like **X-Calibre, X-Factor, X-Terminators, X-Force, X-O Manowar,** and just plain old **X.**

I always wondered what the *X* in X-Men stood for. Was it something cool or mysterious? It turns out that Professor X explained it to Jean Grey when they first met: "You possess an extra power that humans do not! That is why I call my students . . . X-Men, for ex-tra power!"

Well, that was disappointing.

But after extreme athletes started competing in the X Games, we hit a new low. That's about when a superhero named **Adam X the X-Treme** showed up. Adam X wore a backwards baseball cap (like a skater!), had a goatee (like a skater!), and his superpower was the ability to electrify your blood (like a—wait a minute, *what*?).

Hey, if a *letter* can be a superhero name, maybe I should be known as **Brilliant B.** The *B* stands for "Awesome"!

As you can see, superhero names often copy something that's already popular. For example, in 1938, a hero named the **Green Hornet** was famous. So someone invented a new superhero named the **Blue Beetle.** (See what they did there?)

If you're a scientific or magical hero, the title of "Doctor" is a good prescription. Who could disagree with the diagnosis of **Doctor Voodoo, Doctor Strange, Doctor Mid-Nite, Doctor Fate,** or **Doc Savage**?

To get a mysterious name, try spelling a cool word backwards, like the hero known as **El Carim** (*miracle* backwards).

Another possibility is to use the Captain America formula. Just take any military rank (captain, sergeant, major, colonel, etc.) and add the name of the state you live in. Examples: **Captain California, Major Montana, Sergeant South Carolina, Private Pennsylvania, General Georgia, Admiral Alaska,** etc.

Did you know that there've been dozens of superheroes and villains with "Captain" in their names? (And I'm not even counting **Cap'n Crunch.**) Try to spot the "Captain" superhero who I made up below!

Captain Carrot	Captain Everything
Captain Nazi	Captain Fight
Captain Science	Captain Storm
Captain Battle	Captain Caveman
Captain Tootsie	Captain Guts
Captain Unstoppable	Captain Hero

(Give up? See answer below.*)

GREAT MOMENTS IN SUPERHERO NAMES

* Answer: I invented **Captain Unstoppable!**

You may be tempted to use a royal or noble title. But be careful. For some reason, "baron" only works for supervillains. There's **Baron Mordo, Baron Blood, Baron Gestapo, Baron Blitzkrieg,** and the list goes on and on. (Other royal bad guys include **Kingpin** and **Count Dracula.**)

So what's the key to supername success? Try to be original. But more importantly, pick something *catchy* and easy to remember. Otherwise, you'll go to all the trouble of saving the day, and this'll happen.

THE WORST ONE-TWO PUNCH IN HISTORY

A man discovered he had *explosive* power in his fists. So he became the superhero known as the **Human Bomb.** And his sidekick had an even crazier name--**Hustace Throckmorton!**

DON'T BE TOO OBVIOUS

Putting your superpower in your supername doesn't always work. For example, being able to fly is cool, but a superhero named **Fly Girl** sounds dopey. And don't get me started on **Awkwardman!** (He tripped a lot. Really.)

Silly or dramatic names can be good, but don't get *too* cheesy. I mean, have you ever heard of the patriotic crime-fighting duo called **Yank and Doodle**? I think of them as "Yuck and Noodle"!

But I feel sorriest for **Matter-Eater Lad.** Sure, being able to eat rocks or metals is sort of cool, but that *name.* And his official superhero logo is a tooth!

A lot of superheroes just have one tough-sounding name. I like this because it keeps things simple. For example, there's no need to add "Boy" or "Woman" to names like **Zealot, Barricade,** or **Grifter.**

How about you? Any good ideas yet? Not so fast! Before you pick a name, I beg you not to make these . . .

THREE FATAL NAME MISTAKES!

1. Substituting the letter *y* for vowels looks like you're trying too hard. For example, **Insygnia, Bloodwynd,** or **Kyd Flash.** (I mean, a name like **Willy Nilly** is corny but usable. But **Wylly Nylly?** Nah!)

2. Apostrophes usually show possession (example: Superman's turtleneck) or the fact that a letter or letters are missing (isn't = is not). So names like **T'Challa** (the Black Panther), the **Shi'ar** (from the X-Men), or **J'onn J'onzz** (the Martian Manhunter) are confusing!

3. It's a bad idea to smash together little-used letters like *x, q,* and *z.*

Based on these three rules, I just came up with the worst superhero name ever: **Qwyk'sand Wyndzbane!**

Still stuck? Fine, how about this. Try combining words from these two columns—and feel free to use a word from either column first. (Example: **Kid Fancy-Pants.**)

Funky	Person
Literate	Avenger
Crimson	Defender
Fearless	Protector
Stellar	Angel
Epic	Commando
Wicked Awesome	Ace
Amazing	Guardian
Well-Dressed	Thing
Electro-	Beast
Emerald	Titan
Incredible	Kid

Masked	Girl
Radical	Grrrl
Dyna–	Lass
Hazard	Woman
Cool	Lady
Radioactive	Goddess
Killer	Madam
Fancy–Pants	Mademoiselle
Thunder	Boy
Competent	Lad
Black	Man
Rainbow	Dude
Sick	Amigo
Mega	Gentleman
Cosmic	Fella
OK	Guy
Phantom	Bloke
Unreal	Hombre
Impressive	Chap

That wasn't so hard, was it? Of course, you don't need a chart for a good superhero handle. You can bet that Iron Man's enemy **Obadiah Stane** didn't pick his awesome name from this. And neither did the mighty **Afro Samurai.** (Wow!)

YOUR "SECRET" NAME

Let's not forget about the importance of your secret identity name. It's probably your *real* name. But the question is, is your *real* name a good *secret identity* name? (For more on your secret identity, see page 186.)

Here's what I mean: "Bruce" was once a common name, as both **Bruce Wayne** and **Bruce Banner** can tell you. But not anymore—"Bruce" was recently ranked the 532nd most popular name for boy babies.

So that makes "Bruce" stick out in today's world—and that's exactly what you *don't* want! Your secret identity name should blend into the background. If you have a popular name like "Abigail" or "Aidan" or "Sophie" or "Skylar," you're in good shape.

But "Clark" or "Lois"? Not so much. I mean, "Clark" is only the 616th most popular name for boys—and I've never met a "Lois" in my life. Hey, that reminds me! See if you can see what all these names have in common:

Peter Parker

Clark Kent

Bruce Banner

Sue Storm

Reed Richards

Do you see it? These names have first and last names that start with the same *sound.* This sort of thing happens a lot in superhero tales. For example, the Red Bee's alter ego is **Rick Raleigh.** And when I watched the movie *Unbreakable,* I noticed a character named **David Dunn.** (And just *guess* who turns out to be a superhero?)

Sometimes a superhero has an official name *and* a nickname. You know, like **Superman** is also known as the Man of Steel? And **Robin** was called the Boy

* Answer: That's right. They all know Superman!

Wonder. (Embarrassing!) Nicknames can be cool, but don't let yours get too long. For example, the superhero called **Mr. Terrific** was nicknamed "The Human Dynamo Who Is Stumped By Nothing." Wow.

> **HULK MAKE JOKE!** The Hulk likes to call Spider-Man "Bug-Man." Ha! The Hulk also calls Nighthawk "Pointy Nose" and Doctor Strange "Dumb Magician."

Now match the superhero with the correct nickname (see answers below*):

1. Captain America		a.	The Scarlet Speedster
2. Daredevil		b.	Goldilocks
3. The X-Men		c.	Winghead
4. Flash		d.	Shellhead
5. Iron Man		e.	The Man Without Fear
6. Captain Marvel		f.	The Big Red Cheese
7. Thor		g.	Earth's Strangest Superheroes

THE NAME GAME LEADS TO FAME!

Names had a lot to do with Superman's creation. See, the Man of Steel was co-created by a guy named Jerry Siegel. And when Jerry was a little kid, he got teased a lot. On the school playground, kids made fun of his name, yelling, "*Siegel, Siegel, birds of an eagle!*" (I know, it doesn't even make sense.)

* Answers: 1. c; 2. e; 3. g; 4. a; 5. d; 6. f; 7. b.

So little Jerry wished he could just fly away. From an early age, he imagined a fantastic world where people *could* fly. And later, Jerry grew up and invented Superman. And then Superman became so popular, the superhero affected the ways people name their own kids.

For example, actor Nicolas Cage named his son Kal-El. (That's Superman's original name back on Krypton.) And when a Swedish woman named Sara Leisten gave birth, her baby was born with one arm outstretched—like he was flying.

So Sara named her baby "Staalman" (which is the Swedish name for Superman). But a judge rejected this name, saying the baby would get teased if his name was Superman. But you know what's really weird? Sweden was already home to babies with names like Tarzan and Batman!

DRESS LIKE A SUPERHERO!

"I must have a costume that is so bizarre that once I am seen, I will never be forgotten!"

--Green Lantern

You got your start in the superhero business long ago. It began with you tying a towel or blanket around your neck. And then you ran around the house like a maniac with your arms out in front of you and made "swooshing" sounds.

I'm right, huh? After all, that's how *I* got interested in superheroes just last year.

But maybe you're wondering if you *still* need a cape or a special costume. After all, why not just wear your regular clothes? Here's why. Try naming just *one* superhero who wears T-shirts and shorts. See what I mean? And to explain how things got this way, it's time for an . . .

ORIGIN STORY!

Superhero costumes look the way they do because of **circuses.** See, back in the early 1900s, strongmen traveled with circuses and carnivals. The strongmen usually wore tights or long underwear. And over these tights, they put on boots, capes, and colored underpants.

So when superhero creators needed costume ideas, guess who they thought of? Circus strongmen! That's why the very first superhero characters were nicknamed "long underwear heroes." (Of course, circus strongmen also had gigantic mustaches—and luckily, almost no superheroes did.)

> ## Pop Quiz
> *True or false:* The law in Gotham City states that nobody can wear a bat costume except for Batman.*

If you're worried about feeling silly in a bright cape and leotard, think of it as

* Answer: *False!* When Batman tells Batgirl to get rid of her bat costume, she refuses, saying, "The law says no, man, can wear it!"

your *uniform.* It's what you wear when you're out on patrol! So you're no different from the police officer who wears special clothing.

THE RIGHT OUTFIT CAN MAKE YOU INSTANTLY POPULAR!

And speaking of *special,* it's time to talk about . . .

UNDERPANTS!

Unlike the circus strongmen, you can wear your underpants *under* your pants. But for the love of Thor, make sure your underwear's not a bright color, or we'll be able to see it through your costume!

Also, you may ask the classic question: *boxers or briefs?* Let me keep this short—*briefs.* Stuffing boxers under your costume will look *really* dorky. Your butt will look all bumpy and weird, and supervillains will mock you.

You: Stop! In the name of the law!

Villain (chuckling): More like "Stop in the name of lumpy underwear."

You (covering your boxers with your cape): Meanie!

Oh, and please don't let your underwear waistband stick out—unless you want to show off.

AMATEUR NIGHT

Every Halloween, "normal" kids put on capes and masks and act like *they* have superpowers. So on October 31, you'll find children jumping off slides trying to fly, or staring at trees with their "X-ray vision."

There's a word for kids like these: *posers!*

FABRICS!

Pick your costume's material carefully. With your active lifestyle, you want a fabric that breathes well and dries quickly. After all, someone like the Flash is running all the time. That means sweat—*lots* of sweat. So if the Flash's costume doesn't *breathe,* he's really going to stink by the time he gets to a crime scene!

LIGHT-SPEED WRITING: A man named Gardner Fox created the Flash. He also wrote more than 4,000 comic book stories in his career. Writing that fast is hard work--which is why one person described Fox as "the sweatiest man I'd ever met."

Be sure to avoid wool, corduroy, flannel, and pleather costumes. Leather gives good protection, but wearing too much of it makes you look cheesy. So most superhero outfits contain synthetic fabrics like spandex.

I suggest a 50-50-50 blend of spandex, Kevlar, and Nomex. Kevlar is five times stronger than steel, and can stop a bullet. And Nomex is a fire-resistant fabric. So firefighters wear it for protection.

> **WASH AND WEAR:** Get a costume that's easy to wash. (Take it from me, it's really hard to get bloodstains out of your cape!)

What else? Besides being *bulletproof* and *flameproof,* your costume should also be *waterproof* and *laserproof.* But no pressure. (Oh, your fabric should also be *pressure-proof.*)

"YOU WANT PANTS WITH THAT?"

Spider-Man once met a tailor named Leo Zelinsky, who didn't like his costume: "The fabric, I'm guessing spandex. . . . You overheat a lot in this thing, don't you? You've got no weather-proofing, no proper ventilation . . . you could get athlete's foot all over your body in a thing like this."

Zelinsky knew what he was talking about, because he was a *super*tailor. He made costumes for superheroes like Thor and Captain America. But Zelinsky's grandson warned that every costume has limits: "Clothes don't make the heroes. What makes a hero is what happens in your heart."

COLORS!

Don't combine the superpowers of a god with the fashion sense of a preschooler. Let your costume announce who you are with bright colors! Red, orange, green, blue—these colors should be so brilliant people have to wear sunglasses to look at you.

KNOW YOUR COSTUME'S SAFETY INFORMATION!

QUICK CHANGES!

So who's going to *make* your costume? If your superpower is crafting, just do it yourself. Your DIY attitude will impress others.

Impressed Person: Wow, you made that costume yourself? How do you like it?

Crafty Kid: It's sew-sew.

But many heroes leave "craftiness" to the supervillains. (Shazam!) So maybe you need someone else to make your costume. But who? Your butler or sidekick is a good choice. So is any other servant who's hanging around—like one of your parents!

Instruct your costume maker to include as many harnesses, pouches, straps, and buckles as possible.

Oh, and remember that *changing* into a costume can take forever. So to speed things up, you might wear your costume under your regular clothes.

Or just make your regular clothes *reversible!*

MASKS, GOGGLES, AND EYEPATCHES!

When it comes to concealing your identity, nothing beats a mask that covers your face. And think of all the varieties! You can go for the full ski mask style, like Spider-Man. Or maybe you prefer a half-cowl, like Batman?

If you don't like masks, try hiding your face with a hood, a handkerchief, or even a big hat. But I don't suggest using a cardboard box with eyeholes cut into it. (Mine always gets spun around during fights.)

PRO TIP: Batman covers the eyeholes of his mask with a one-way fabric. He can still see fine, but nobody can see his eyes. (Spooky!)

Sunglasses and goggles can also give you a different look. So break out your ski goggles—or just make your own!

SUPERPOWER ACTIVITY
SUPERGOGGLES!

Supplies: Pencil, paper, sharp scissors or X-Acto knife, duct tape, large colored plastic soft drink bottle.

1. Sketch a real-size outline on paper of the kind of goggles you want. Remember, unlike glasses, goggles usually wrap around the head.

continued

2. Cut it out and hold
    it up to your face to
    make sure it's about
    the right size. Redo if
    necessary.

3. Tape the paper model
    around the soft drink
    bottle.

4. Carefully cut around it.
    (Have an adult, butler, or sidekick do this.)

5. Try it on! You may need
    to duct-tape the two
    arms together in the back
    to get the goggles to stay
    on. Or punch holes at the
    two ends of the goggles.
    Then tie and knot some
    string between the holes
    to help keep the glasses
    in place.

One more thing—eyepatches aren't very practical, but they *do* look cool. Just ask famous eyepatcher **Nick Fury.** He works for S.H.I.E.L.D. (Strategic Homeland Intervention, Enforcement, and Logistics Division).

Years ago, I got a summer job at S.H.I.E.L.D. headquarters. One day I was in the crime lab and I accidentally knocked over a glass beaker. At first I thought I'd be in trouble. But Nick Fury just turned a blind eye to my accident. (Shazam!)

But in honor of Fury, I started wearing an eyepatch—and you may want to do the same thing.

ACCESSORIES!

There are an endless number of accessories available for today's superhero. But choose ones that are fashionable *and* practical. For example, **Wonder Woman's** bracelets. Sure, they look good—but those wristbands also save lives!

Wonder Woman's bracelets are made from a metal called "amazonium." They can stop bullets, lasers, and even artillery. (**Fun Fact:** Wonder Woman's tiara is made of the same stuff. Sometimes she throws it like a boomerang!) But amazonium is rare. So here's an alternative way to get the same look!

SUPERPOWER ACTIVITY
POWER BANDS!

Supplies: Scissors, toilet paper rolls, blue painter's tape, bright paint, glue, glitter.

1. Cut the toilet paper roll once, from top to bottom. Then cut it in *half.* You should have two pieces that look like the picture.

2. Close the rolls and tape them shut on the *inside.*

continued

3. Stuff the rolls with newspaper. Also, lay down some newspaper on your worktable for the next part.

4. Paint the power bands. Let them dry.

5. Lightly add glue to the paint. Now add your glitter!

   Optional: After this dries, paint a glaze of two parts water, one part glue over the bracelets.

6. If you have any power stones or precious gems, glue these to the power bands.

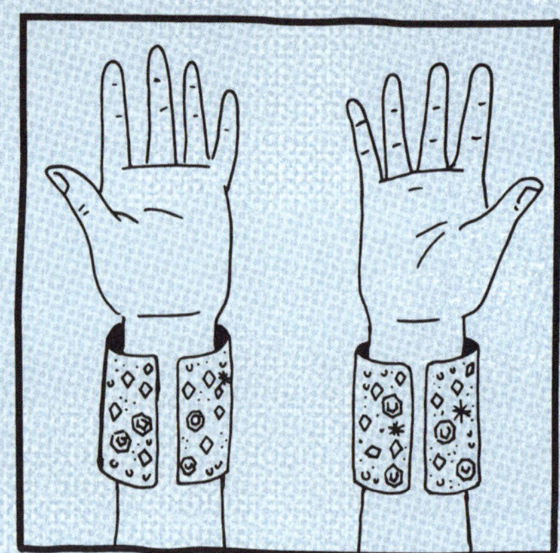

7. After they're dry, remove the newspaper and painter's tape from inside the rolls.

8. Slip on the power bands and go fight crime!

UTILITY BELT!

Superheroes carry a *lot* of gadgets. So you need a wide nylon belt with containers called a **utility belt.** Think of it as a fanny pack with *lots* of packs. (That's better than lots of *fannies*!)

So, what should you keep in your utility belt? Good choices include:

Flashlight

First aid kit

Swiss Army knife

Binoculars

The Ultimate Gadget

What's that? You've never heard of the *Ultimate Gadget?*

SUPERPOWER ACTIVITY

THE ULTIMATE GADGET!

Supplies: Old cell phone, silver or gold spray paint, glitter (optional).

If you carry just one gadget on your utility belt, it should be this one. Here's how to make it:

1. Get an old cell phone.

2. Spray paint it silver. Or gold. Feel free to stick glitter on it, too.

3. Let it dry.

Now, what do you do with this thing? Hey, the only limitation to your gadget is your imagination! Use it as a communication device, weapon, prop, or even toothpick! (Okay, maybe not a toothpick.)

Don't worry about your belt running out of storage space for your gadgets. I mean, **Batman's** utility belt holds an amazing amount of stuff. Just try to guess which item Batman *doesn't* keep in his belt:

Crayons

A tiny blowtorch

Shark repellent

Nylon ties (used for handcuffs)

Kryptonite

An extra Batman costume

A makeup kit

The Batcopter

Batarangs

Did you guess the Batcopter? Good job! All of the other items really *are* in Batman's belt. (He even keeps Kryptonite in case Superman messes with him.) But of all Batman's gadgets, the **batarangs** are my favorite. These small metal weapons shaped like bats are designed for throwing. They're sort of like combination throwing stars and boomerangs.

Batman also has specialized batarangs. These include a Seeing-Eye batarang (with a camera), a fire-prevention batarang (loaded with fire-extinguishing chemicals), and even a bomb batarang (*ka-boom!*). How great would it be to have your own "-arangs"? Let's just say that I always carry my own *Bart-arangs*: small metal boomerangs shaped like me.

And now you're probably wondering if I drive a car called the *Bart*mobile. Of course not! (That would just be silly.)

FOUR FANTASTIC COSTUME PROBLEMS FROM THE FANTASTIC FOUR!

1. **The Human Torch and His Flaming Underwear:** If the Human Torch's skin is covered with fire, how come he still has a costume on when the flame goes out?

2. **The Invisible Girl and Her Disappearing Costume:** One of Sue Storm's superpowers is turning invisible. Fair enough! But why, oh *why*, does her outfit turn invisible too?

3. **The Fantastic Mr. Stretch Pants:** Mr. Fantastic can stretch and stretch and s-t-r-e-t-c-h … and his *costume* can too! Reed Richards explains that he did this by making the costume out of "unstable molecules." (This is a good catchall excuse: "Why did you spill the milk?" "Unstable molecules!")

4. **Wild Thing:** Actually, the guy made of bricks has the most realistic costume of the bunch: Blue short shorts!

CAPES!

"No capes."

—Edna Mode, The Incredibles

You know why capes are forbidden, right? They're *dangerous*. After all, who wants to get sucked into a jet aircraft engine? But despite that, there is *one* really good reason to wear a cape:

It looks cool!

See what I mean? A cape may not be practical, but it will bring you *respect.* Plus, if you're a little skinny or chunky, it can help hide that.

But what size should your cape be? It should hang down to the back of your knees. But not any longer, or you'll trip on it. And no shorter than your beltline, or it'll just look silly!

You also want the cape to be roomy—but not *so* big that it looks like you're wearing a tarp. BTW, I know what you're thinking: that you're too cool to make a cape by stuffing a blanket under your collar. But are you kidding? Capes made from blankies are the best kind!

ATOMIC WEDGIE!

The **Atom** is a superhero who shrinks down to a tiny size. When the Atom shrinks, his normal "street clothes" vanish and his superhero costume appears. Then, after the Atom grows back to his usual size, his everyday clothes cover him again--but his superhero costume stays *small*! So according to scientist James Kakalios, that means "the Atom is the only superhero who deliberately gives himself a wedgie whenever he returns to his secret identity!"

EXOSKELETON

Exo- just means "outside." So an exoskeleton is something you wear on the *outside* of your body. It might be a costume with light armor, like Batman's batsuit. Or it can be an actual robot that you *wear.* For example, Tony Stark puts on a full-body, robotic exoskeleton to become **Iron Man.**

There are lots of good reasons to wear an exoskeleton. It can give you defense against fists, bullets, and even explosions. And a good exoskeleton can actually make you stronger and faster! But it does have drawbacks.

THREE EXOSKELETON PROBLEMS

1. Your batteries can run down awfully fast! (Tony Stark has crawled around looking for an electrical outlet to plug into when his suit's power got low.)

2. An exoskeleton gives you *two* skeletons to worry about— the one *inside* of you and the one *outside* of you. (That's just weird!)

3. How do you go to the bathroom in an exoskeleton? (Actually, never mind. I don't want to know!)

IRON MAN!

Tony Stark is a guy whose only superpower is his *mind.* But that's enough! Because Stark is a genius, he invents his own suit of electronic armor. With the suit he can do things like fly, shoot force beams, and use superstrength.

He becomes Iron Man!

Tony Stark's very first Iron Man suit was gray. But luckily his girlfriend asked, "If [Iron Man's] a modern knight in shining armor, why doesn't he wear *golden* armor?" So Tony Stark changed the exoskeleton's colors.

Now here's another good question: Does Tony Stark *wear* his suit? Or *drive* it? (Or fly it? Or ride it?)

Tony Stark has invented different special armored suits over time. These suits have mysterious names and uses that we can only guess at, like:

The Hulkbuster

Arctic Armor

War Machine

The Thorbuster

Space Armor

BTW, one of Tony Stark's overlooked abilities is **multitasking.** That means he can do more than one thing at a time. For comparison, you can walk and chew gum at the same time. If you concentrate, you can also rub your stomach with one hand while doing this.

But what if you try to:

1. Walk

2. Chew gum

3. Rub your stomach with one hand

4. . . . and tap your head with your *other* hand?

For most people, that's one too many tasks. And your brain just sort of gives up. So if you're not careful, you'll:

1. Fall down

2. Swallow your gum

3. Punch yourself in the stomach as you land

4. . . . and look really silly!

But for about 3 percent of all people, doing that would be easy. That's because they're so good at multitasking they are "supertaskers." For example, Tony Stark can fly at 400 mph, listen to music, talk to Pepper Potts, shoot repulsor rays, and watch his suit's monitors all at once. That makes Iron Man a *supertasking superhero.*

MAGICAL PANTS!

One of the only superheroes without a costume is the Incredible Hulk. After all, let's say that Bruce Banner got angry and ripped through all his clothes. Why would he turn into the Hulk and appear in a brand-new outfit?

So instead of a costume, the Hulk's got green skin. Even so, he *still* has a clothing problem. Because when the hulking Hulk bursts out of his clothes, he's *still* wearing pants! Sure they get torn a bit, but that's it. And in his early adventures, the Hulk always had *purple* pants, no matter what clothes Bruce Banner had been wearing.

He had "magical pants"!

WHAT'S THIS "RIGHT VS. WRONG" STUFF?!

Dude, you're famous. All superheroes are! But as a celebrity, you're going to be under a microscope.

No, not *literally*—unless you have the power to shrink. What I mean is that people watch superheroes like us very closely. And they think we're all total goody-goodys, like **Captain America.** Talk about pressure! That means if you do even *one* little bad thing (like jaywalking) people will think you're *totally* evil.

This is one of the hardest things about being a superhero: The bar is set *really* high! But that's okay. You can just fly right over it!

What the public doesn't understand is that superheroes are all *different* from each other. So what type of hero do *you* want to be? Maybe it's your dream to be a *funny* superhero. Or perhaps you prefer being thought of as a *reluctant* superhero, or even a *six-toed* superhero.

One popular choice is the *antihero* superhero. This is any character who's too *good* to be a villain, but too *bad* to be a normal superhero. (Think of **Wolverine, Venom,** and **Lobo.**)

POP QUIZ

EASY SCIENCE!

True or False: Wolverine's claws could cut through Captain America's shield.

(See answer below.*)

* *Answer: False!* Everyone knows that adamantium claws can't cut a steel/vibranium alloy.

To help you pick the right style, think of the game called *Dungeons & Dragons*. Every character in *D&D* is one of three types: **Good, Neutral,** or **Evil.** Of course, Good and Evil types are easy to understand. And Neutral means the character might do good *or* bad things, depending on the situation.

Within each of those three categories are three subcategories: **Lawful, Neutral,** and **Chaotic.** Lawful characters are honest and follow the rules. Chaotic characters hate authority and do what they want. And Neutral characters fall somewhere between those two.

Obviously, you're not going to be Evil. But now we can see that being Good (or even Neutral) can be complicated!

WHERE DO YOU WANT TO BE?

LAWFUL GOOD:	NEUTRAL GOOD:	CHAOTIC GOOD:
Captain America, Superman	Wonder Woman, Green Lantern	Spider-Man, Batman
LAWFUL NEUTRAL: Megamind, William Stryker	**NEUTRAL:** Swamp Thing, Hellboy	**CHAOTIC NEUTRAL:** Deadpool, the Hulk, Catwoman
LAWFUL EVIL: Magneto, Ra's al Ghul	**NEUTRAL EVIL:** Doctor Doom, Mystique, Galactus	**CHAOTIC EVIL:** The Joker, Carnage

The rules of what's right and wrong are called **ethics.** And as a "good guy" (or at least a "neutral guy") you need to be ethical. But ethics can take a lot of thought, because the right thing to do is not always clear. Yep, ethics can be as slippery as a supervillain covered in toothpaste!

Oh, ick.

Anyway, here's an example. Let's say that *you* can fly, but your best friend is afraid of heights. So you try to be helpful!

We all know that's not ethical, right? Right! Now let's look at a trickier situation. One time the **Human Torch** was fighting a guy named **Plantman**. And Plantman was tough! First he threw wet acorns at the Human Torch. Then Plantman turned on a sprinkler, putting out the Torch's flames. Talk about annoying!

The Human Torch was pretty sure that Plantman was a bad guy. And the superhero *really* wanted to win that fight. So the Human Torch sprayed a container of weed killer all over Plantman.

Did the Human Torch go too far? Maybe! But as a superhero, you will also be faced with ethical questions like, "How badly do I want to win?" and "Did I just kill Plantman?"

SUPER USEFUL INFORMATION! The average surface temperature of the Human Torch is 780°F. Okay, I lied about that being "useful." (How unethical!)

When it comes to ethics, there are no easy answers. Your best bet is to let your conscience be your guide. And then do the right thing! For more pointers, let's look at some **ethical FAQs:**

Q. Is it okay for me to join my school's sports teams even though I have superpowers?

A. There was once a kid named Clark Kent who was the best athlete at his school. (He was also the best athlete in the *world.*) But because of ethics, he chose not to play football. Clark thought, "I could be the world's greatest football player, [but] it would be unfair to win that way."

But there are exceptions. If you can breathe underwater, it'd be wrong for you to join your school's swim team. (You'd have an unfair advantage.) But it would fine for you to be on the chess team— just as long as the matches aren't played underwater.

Q. A supervillain just shot my grandmother with a "wet-noodle ray." Then he ran off! Should I chase the villain or help my grandmother?

A. This is a tricky one. If you go after the villain, your grandmother could slip into a wet-noodle coma. But if you help *her,* the culprit escapes—and he might do the same thing to someone else. It's a real dilemma!

Q. Yeah, I knew that already. But what should I *do*?

A. Hang on—I just got another question!

Q. Let's say I was in PE class when a giant meteorite hit City Hall. Would it be okay for me to cut school and go help?

A. It depends. If your PE class is doing a ballroom dance unit, then you really should go help. But if your PE teacher scheduled a tug-of-war followed by a pizza party . . . well, I'm sure those people at City Hall will be just fine!

Q. Can I do something *bad* if it leads to a greater *good*? For instance, what if my little brother sprained his ankle on an airport runway? As he lies there, a huge jet hurtles toward him. If I don't stop the jet with my superstrength, my little brother will get squished. But if I *do* stop the jet, hundreds of people might die from the impact!

A. Tell your little brother to stop goofing around at the airport.

Q. I caught a bank robber this weekend. After tying him up and calling the police, I noticed there were millions of dollars just lying around. Would it be okay if I stuffed a few bills in my underwear? After all, I bet nobody would miss the cash. And I sort of earned it!

A. You say *nobody* would know if you took some cash. But *one* person would know: *you.* And remember, your conscience is your best guide with ethical problems. (Also? It's totally unethical to spend money after stuffing it in your underwear.)

THE MAN OF STEAL?

Superman might be the most honest superhero ever--but even *he's* broken some rules! I mean, think about this--Superman is totally *rich.* He's always collecting reward money, discovering treasure, and squeezing coal into diamonds.

But does Superman ever pay any taxes? *No.* And that's not ethical. *Everybody* has to pay taxes! So that's why Superman once got a bill for *one billion dollars* in unpaid taxes. Yikes.

So Superman came up with a plan. You see, parents pay less money in taxes because they have kids. Their children are called "dependents." That's because the kids *depend* on their Mom and Dad for support.

So Superman declared every person on Earth a "dependent." After all, he'd saved the planet many times over. And with billions of dependents, Superman's tax debt was wiped away!

Moral: Saving the planet makes good financial sense.

As you can see, ethics can be hard to understand. But you can handle it! After all, as a superhero, you're smarter and better than everybody else. So why should you have to follow the same rules as "normal" people?

Heck, you should be their *ruler.* Am I right?

No, no, no. I'm *wrong*! Thinking like that only leads to trouble. Don't be an egomaniac! And remember, you're no better than all the boring, sad, ordinary people out there.

Keeping this in mind takes *self-control.* Just think of the last time someone made you mad. Maybe you saw some maniac speeding on his tricycle! Sure, you're tempted to blast the *driver.* But it's more ethical to disable his *vehicle.*

Sadly, getting revenge on normal people is not ethical. This is true for the same reason that you don't push around little kids (even if they deserve it!). Just because you're a superhero doesn't mean you get to be a *bully*.

So now you have a better idea of ethics, right? If not, just pretend. (That's what I do!)

YOUR SECRET IDENTITY

A good way to stay in touch with average people is your **secret identity.** (It's also called an "alter ego" or "double identity.") But some of you may not need a secret identity. If you're a weird-looking mutant—like the Thing—forget about it. Disguises don't work! What are you going to do, lie down on a brick patio and disappear? (Shazam!)

BTW, if you *are* a weird-looking mutant, that's *great*. Please don't hurt me! But if you're *not*, be sure to read the next section.

FOUR RULES FOR YOUR SECRET IDENTITY

1. **Secrecy!** Keep your secret identity a *secret.* Otherwise, it's just a *regular* identity, and that's not as impressive. And don't get tricked into telling anyone who you are!

By the way, the secrecy rule applies to your superpowers, too. You don't want to tell anyone what your superpowers are—or *aren't.*

Criminal: What kinds of superpowers do you have?

Otter Boy: Besides being good at catching fish, I really don't have any!

Criminal (pulling out a baseball bat): In that case, would you mind holding still?

2. **Keep Track!** Your *secret identity* is your "normal" life. You know, the one you had before becoming a superhero? So when Bruce Wayne wakes up in the morning, he's *Bruce Wayne.* When Peter Parker pours milk on his cereal, he's *Peter Parker.* It's not until these two put on their costumes that they become Batman and Spider-Man. So just to make it clear:

SUPERHERO	SECRET IDENTITY
Batman	Bruce Wayne
Spider-Man	Peter Parker

But it's different if you're *born* a superhero. When Superman gets up in the morning, he's *Superman.* He has to put on a "costume" to become Clark Kent! Weird, huh?

The superheroes with the trickiest secret identities are
the X-Men. Most of them started life as "normal" human
beings. But during their teen years, mutants' superpowers
develop. Then the X-Men face a question: "Do I keep my
original identity 'secret' or not?"

3. **Nerdiness!** Your secret identity must be nerdy. It's a law!
So Catwoman's a librarian. Clark Kent wears glasses.* And
Peter Parker is a clueless bookworm. He's even described
as someone who "wouldn't know a cha-cha from a waltz."

Hey, wait a minute—neither do I!

Anyway, being a goofball misfit is the perfect cover for your
superpowers. Who would guess that the kid with all the
multisided dice is actually Power Dude?

YOUR BASIC SUPERHERO

* Clark Kent's also able to hypnotize people to not notice that he looks *exactly* like Superman.

To make your nerd camouflage perfect:

- Spill things. A lot! Then try to wipe up the mess with something silly, like small tissues or your socks.

- Carry lots of folders. Then trip over your feet and send your papers flying.

- Bump into people and mutter, "I beg your pardon," while pushing your glasses up your nose.

- Wear glasses. (Or that previous tip won't work!)

- If someone mentions your superhero identity, act like you're terrified of him. ("Yes, I've heard of Vomit Lad. And boy, does he give me the shivers!")

> **NERDS!** The nerdiest superhero was a brainy clone of the Hulk. Known as **Nerd Hulk,** he was supersmart and never got angry. And guess what? It turned out that Nerd Hulk was a gigantic wuss. (Even Captain America could beat him up!)

4. **Career Choice!** If you're a kid, having a secret identity is easier than you think. That's because everyone thinks you're at school all day. And of course, that's where you *usually* are . . . if you're not fighting crime!

But as you get older, you'll need a job. Rats! So think about working as a reporter. That way, you can disappear for hours "working on a story" and no one will be suspicious. Just look at Peter Parker. He sells news photographs to the newspaper called the *Daily Bugle.*

There is a catch, though. Like superheroes, reporters have rules. And Peter often breaks one of these rules. See, Peter sometimes takes photos of Spider-Man. But Peter *is* Spider-Man. That's a problem! Reporters have an ethical duty to *report* the news—but not *make* the news.

Clark Kent does the same thing. Whether writing for newspapers, TV, or the Internet, Clark Kent reports on Superman all the time. But he never tells people that he *is* Superman. That's just not right. So remember, after you become a reporter, don't write about yourself!

I know this whole "secret identity" thing sounds like a lot of work. And there are rare superheroes who *don't* have a secret identity. You know, like Wolverine? He's *always* a superhero. There's a name for characters like this: show-offs.

And speaking of show-offs, why does **Aquaman** think he's so great? It must be because he's . . .

THE ONLY SUPERHERO WITH A GAS BLADDER?

Kid (concerned): Aquaman, start swimming! If you don't deactivate those underwater missiles, we're all doomed!

Aquaman: I have to wait a half hour first.

Kid (outraged): Why?!

Aquaman: I just ate a hard-boiled egg. And you should always wait thirty minutes before . . .

As a crime-fighting merman, Aquaman's been out there treading water since 1941. He's not the most popular superhero, but Aquaman's not all washed up either. What's the secret to his survival? It's simple:

Sometimes, you just *really* need someone who can talk to a fish.

And Aquaman has a big heart. There's more than twenty thousand species of fish—and Aquaman cares about them all. That's why he started an undersea hospital for sea creatures.

This hospital came in handy the time that Aquaman got shot. While lantern fish provided light for the operation, suckerfish sucked out the bullets from the superhero's wound. And a nurse shark even took care of him! (Okay, I made that last bit up.)

Aquaman can swim down to any depth. Of course, fish dive down all the time. That's because fish have a gas bladder that holds air. If the fish wants to dive down, it leaks air from its bladder. If the fish wants to rise up, it *adds* air to its bladder.

So Aquaman must do the same thing. And that means he's probably the only superhero with a gas bladder!

HEAVYWEIGHT HERO: To survive beneath the ocean's great pressures, Aquaman's body is superdense. So he weighs 325 pounds!

SUPERVILLAINS AND OTHER ETHICALLY CHALLENGED PEOPLE!

As a superhero, you need three things:

- A costume

- A secret identity

- An archenemy

That's right, an enemy! What else are you going to do if you're not fighting evildoers? "*Right wrongs*"? Bor-ring.

Luckily for you, the world is chock-full of bad guys. It turns out that there are *dozens* of villains for every superhero. And sometimes these criminals are awfully easy to spot.

SPOT THE SUPERVILLAIN!

But the sneakier villains are harder to identify. To practice, try spotting the supervillains you meet in your day-to-day life. Once you start looking, you'll find these annoying people are everywhere. You know, like the mean waiter at the restaurant who says, "You can only order off the kids' menu."

But is just being *annoying* enough to be considered *evil*?

YES.

As your evil-spotting skills improve, you'll learn something interesting. Most people aren't *all* good or *all* bad. Green Lantern learned this the hard way when he said to his power ring, "Get rid of all the evil that is plaguing mankind!"

Suddenly, *everyone* on Earth disappeared—because everyone has *some* evil inside.

So take a look in the mirror. Are you actually a good person? Or is it just possible you could somehow become a villain? Maybe all it would take for you to turn to the dark side is . . .

ONE TERRIBLE, HORRIBLE, NO-GOOD, VERY BAD DAY

Many villains were once normal, everyday citizens. Take Harvey Dent. He worked for law and order, and called Batman his friend. But then Harvey had a terrible, horrible, no-good, very bad day.* And after something terrible happened to Harvey, he became something *terrible*. Namely, Harvey became the villain known as **Two-Face.**

But what other kinds of awful events could drive a normal person to crime? You'd be surprised.

At breakfast: *"My pancakes are soggy."*

At lunch: *"This sandwich got smushed."*

At dinner: *"Peas?"*

Result: *"I will destroy the world!"*

Some people need more than *one* bad day to turn bad. Scientist Otto Octavius broke up with his girlfriend. Then he saw his mom die. Finally, Otto suffered an accident in the lab. So no wonder he became the feared **Doctor Octopus!**

Of course, of all the "One Bad Day" villains, one is more famous than all the others combined.

* If you must know, someone threw acid in his face.

THE JOKER

Nicknames: The Fiendish Funster, the Clown Prince of Crime, the Grinning Gargoyle of Greed, the Harlequin of Hate, the Mad Maestro of Mirth.

Former Identity: He once called himself "John Dough."

Superpowers: Insanity. (Plus, he's mean!)

Biography: At the beginning of his criminal career, the **Joker** was chased by Batman into a playing card company. There, he jumped into a chemical vat to escape. Oops! The chemicals dyed his skin white, his hair green, and his lips red. And they dyed his brain *insane*. (Talk about a bad day!)

FUN FACTS: The Joker was supposed to be a "one-shot" villain who died and never appeared again. In his first appearance, the Joker murdered someone and stole a big diamond. So Robin tried hard to get Batman to pursue the criminal.

"Not yet," Batman answered. "The time isn't ripe."
(Uh . . . when *will* it be ripe?)

Superpower Activity

Get into the Mind of a Supervillain!

Supplies: Chessboard, action figures, acting ability.

Want to get into the head of a supervillain? Then try *acting* like one.

1. Buy or make some superhero action figures.

2. Put the action figures on a chessboard. See? They're all just pawns in your evil game.

3. Now move the pieces around on the board and talk *to* yourself *about* yourself. Remember to cackle and make boastful threats.

Hey, have you ever noticed how many of Batman's enemies are insane? **Two-Face,** the **Scarecrow, Poison Ivy,** the **Joker,** the **Riddler, Bane** . . . it's *crazy.* And that reminds me of the next supervillain category—

THE MAD SCIENTIST

Obsessed researchers. Dangerous experiments. White lab coats.

These are all signs of a mad scientist. But what causes a scientist to go mad in the first place? Is it all that science homework?

Maybe! But often these villains just want to get revenge. (Most James Bond villains are like that.) Also, most mad scientists make the exact same mistake— they experiment on *themselves.* For example, there was a one-armed scientist named Dr. Curtis Connors. He wanted to help people grow back missing limbs.

Since lizards can grow back their tails, Connors used lizards for his research. Then he developed a special serum—and took it himself! (And of course Dr. Connors was alone when he did this.)

The *good news* was that Connors' serum worked. He grew his arm back!

The *bad news* was he turned into a giant, insane, talking lizard. So his experiment had its pluses and minuses. Anyway, the mad scientist known as the **Lizard** became one of Spider-Man's archenemies.

MY TWO FAVORITE MAD SCIENTISTS: The supervillain called **Arsenal** has an awesome secret identity name: **Nimrod Strange.** (No wonder he's angry!) And scientist Wilbur Day committed crimes using "power stilts" that extended up to three hundred feet. So he was known as **Stilt-Man.**

HIGH SCHOOL STUDENTS

If you have an older sibling, you know how easily teenagers can become evil. Take Edward Nigma. He was an average high school student until his school held a jigsaw puzzle–solving contest that Edward won by cheating. So his lesson was that crime *does* pay. And that's how "E. Nigma" started down the road of becoming the Riddler. **Moral:** Never enter school contests. They lead to a life of crime!

IT'S LIFE OR DEATH! The Riddler likes to trap superheroes in puzzles––and here's one now! Imagine being locked in a room with six buttons in front of you. Each button has a letter on it: *A, B, C, D, E,* and *F.* You hear a voice: "Pick the letter that is most like death. If you pick the wrong one, you *die!*" Which button should you push?*

MATCH THE SUPERVILLAIN WITH HIS ARCHENEMY!

1. The Red Skull   a. The Fantastic Four

2. The Beagle Boys   b. Captain America

3. Doctor Doom   c. Wonder Woman

4. Kingpin   d. Uncle Scrooge

5. Mars   e. Daredevil

(See answers below.†)

† Answers: **1. b; 2. d; 3. a; 4. e; 5. c.**

* The correct answer is E. (That's because E comes at the end of LIFE!)

MISUNDERSTOOD VILLAINS

Strangely, we sometimes root for bad guys and girls. Somehow they get our sympathy! Think of **Magneto,** the Master of Magnetism. He was born as Erik Lehnsherr to a Jewish family in the late 1920s. After World War II started, the Nazis imprisoned young Erik in a concentration camp. There he realized:

1. Small groups are always in danger from large groups.
2. He was a mutant who could move metal.

Sadly, Erik's friends and family were all killed. So after Erik became Magneto and said, "I have wept over too many graves," you have to feel bad for him. (And that also explains why Magneto wants to *protect* mutants from the humans.)

> **FUN FACT:** Although Magneto can destroy skyscrapers, you could hit him pretty easily with a wooden baseball bat.

THE ENEMY COMMANDER

Sometimes a supervillain just wants to *conquer* everyone. You know, like **Darth Vader** in *Star Wars,* or the evil Nazi named the **Red Skull.** He was second-in-command to Adolf Hitler during World War II.

How bad *was* the Red Skull? **Captain America** said the Red Skull liked to "revel in atrocity! Bask in evil! Delight in depravity!"

So that's pretty bad.

What's funny is that Captain America had a fan club called the Sentinels of Liberty. Its members were expected to help Captain America in any way they could. So during World War II, hundreds of kids in the fan club reported their friends and neighbors to the police as enemy "spies." But of course, these people were totally innocent. (Kids! You've got to love them.)

SUPERPOWER ACTIVITY
POWER RAY TAG!

Supplies: Three or more players, one power
ray transmitter (a.k.a. "a flashlight").

Power Ray Tag can only be played at night. And *where* you
play has to be a safe place to run around without being
destroyed. (So abandoned mine shafts and warehouses are a
bad idea.)

1. Select a player who will be the *superhero.* He or
    she will try to catch the other players . . . who
    are all *villains,* of course!

2. There needs to be a *jail* where the "caught" villains
    are locked up. (This can just be a tree that they
    have to stand by.)

3. The superhero goes to a spot and starts counting
    to fifty. Meanwhile, the villains scatter. (But not
    too far!)

4. The superhero turns on his power ray transmitter
    and begins the search. If she spots a villain,
    she has to flash the person with the power ray
    transmitter and call the person's name. (Example:
    "I see you, Arachnid-Man!") The villain then goes
    to jail.

5. The last player to be discovered gets to be the
    superhero in the next round!

ARTIFICIAL VILLAINS

Sometimes, evildoers are too busy to commit crimes themselves. So they build substitute villains! Take **Brainiac.** This green-skinned android was made by aliens on a distant planet. (An "android" is an artificial human.) Brainiac is incredibly intelligent. He's basically an evil computer who can walk around and make trouble.

For example, Brainiac shrank an entire city down and stuck the whole thing in a jar. And there were still real people in it and everything! (Uncool, Brainiac. Uncool.)

* A synthezoid.

2. Underneath the supervillain's toilet seats are two small knobs or ridges. These rest on the porcelain rim of the toilet. Place the cut-out bits of bubble wrap under these knobs. Gently lower the toilet seat onto them.

3. Make sure the bubble wrap isn't sticking out or looking suspicious.

4. Wait. When the supervillain goes into the bathroom and sits on the seat, there will be two loud *pops!*

5. Watch the supervillain flee your city, never to return. (And be sure to dispose of the bubble wrap properly.)

ALIENS

Some visitors from other worlds are peaceful. But others, like **Thanos,** just want to fight superheroes and make trouble for Earthlings. And of these aliens, there's one who's so powerful even Superman can't defeat him!

He's **Mr. Mxyzptlk,** an imp from the fifth dimension. (I guess they don't have vowels in the fifth dimension!) Since Mr. Mxyzptlk comes from a different dimension, Superman's superpowers are no use against him. As for the little imp with the big name, he can float on air, bring objects to life, become invisible, and teleport anywhere.

THAT'S RIGHT: The first thing Mr. Mxyzptlk ever said was, "Confusing, aren't I?"

Like all imps, Mr. Mxyzptlk is mischievous. But Superman discovers a way to stop this troublemaker. You just have to get Mr. Mxyzptlk to say his own name backwards. Then he goes back to the fifth dimension.

For the record, that's "Kltpzyxm." (And if *you* can say that out loud, you get to go to another dimension too!*)

NEMATODE ALERT! Captain Marvel's archenemy was the mysterious **Mr. Mind.** Nobody knew *who* this villain was. But eventually Mr. Mind was revealed to be . . . a worm.

* Here, I'll give you a hint—it's pronounced *kel-tip-zix-um.* (Seeya!)

SUPERVILLAIN TEAMS

What's the only thing worse than an insane criminal with superpowers? *Twenty* insane criminals with superpowers!

My favorite supervillain team is the **F-Men.** This was a bunch of kids who were kidnapped by an evil genius. First, the genius turned the kids into versions of their favorite superhero characters. Yay! And then he made them commit crimes. Boo!

The F-Men were obviously a take-off on the X-Men. So see if you can match up these F-Men with their X-Men counterparts. (See answers below.*)

<table>
<tr><td>

1. *Drizzle* makes bad weather.
2. *Clodhoppus* can turn into concrete.
3. The *Weasel* grows "petulantium" fangs.
4. *Slimesquirmer* can teleport--and make milk go sour!
5. *Airhead* passes through solid objects.
6. *Zitpops* can pop his mutant pimples in destructive blasts!

</td><td>

a. Nightcrawler
b. Cyclops
c. Storm
d. Ariel
e. Colossus
f. Wolverine

</td></tr>
</table>

THE SPECIALIZED VILLAIN

Some villains have very specific skills—like the **Top.** His superpower revolves around spinning things, like whirlwinds and tornadoes. The Top also liked to spin *himself* around really fast. He insisted the "spinning action increases my brain power!"

Really? Let me try.

* Answers: 1. c; 2. e; 3. f; 4. a; 5. d; 6. b.

starts spinning

Whoa, I must be doing *something* wrong! Because this is only increasing my *barfing* power. ☹

FOUR REASONS PEOPLE BECOME SUPERVILLAINS

Even though it's evil and stuff, the carefree life of a supervillain can be awfully tempting. Here's why:

1. ***It's Fun!*** Besides Tony Stark, most superheroes don't enjoy themselves. Instead, they're always worrying about doing the "right thing." Supervillains, on the other hand, are having a *great* time. They don't have to worry about playing by the rules. Know why? *THERE ARE NO RULES.*

   Just look at Thor's brother **Loki.** He's the god of mischief. That sounds like a *lot* of fun. And think of the **Joker**--he's got a smile and a kind word for everyone!

   Well, a smile anyway.

2. ***Supervillains Don't Get Picked On!*** Who wants to say something mean to an evil mastermind? Anyone? Anyone?

   That's what I thought.

3. ***Convenience!*** Villains don't usually bother with a secret identity. That's because embracing the dark side is a full-time job.

SHAZAM! Darth Vader made me toast once. (But it was a little on the dark side.)

4. *Power!* Sure, helping people has its rewards. But once you have the power to crush the Earth in your fist, these three words make being a supervillain totally worth it: *free frozen yogurt.*

FRIEND OR FOE?

GENESIS OF A SUPERVILLAIN: Long ago, tales were told of **Grendel,** a horrible villain feared for his attacks on the local castle. Why was Grendel so mean? Because the happy singing from the castle really annoyed him!

THE CRIMINAL MASTERMIND

Does your school have a Gifted and Talented Program? If so, it may have a criminal mastermind who's directing some complex and evil scheme.

The most famous mastermind is Superman's nemesis, **Lex Luthor.** As a teenager, Lex lived in Smallville and became friends with young Clark Kent.

But their friendship went downhill after Lex got caught in a science lab fire. During the fire he inhaled bad stuff like kryptonite dust and radiation. Clark Kent blew the fire out with his superbreath, but it was too late: the chemicals and radiation make Lex Luthor go *bald.*

And he was just a kid. Bummer!

Lex's teenage baldness turned him into a criminal mastermind. (That's what baldness can do to a person!) But while Lex is bad, he *isn't* bloodthirsty. See, he doesn't actually want to *kill* Superman. Instead, he likes tricking the Man of Steel. Then while Superman is confused, Lex puts his evil schemes into action.

Amazingly, Lex Luthor also does *good* deeds. He's donated millions of dollars to charity. And Luthor once saved an entire planet from destruction! Its people were so happy they renamed the planet Lexor in his honor. How nice!

Then later, Lex Luthor accidentally destroyed Lexor. (That's *not* nice.)

THE "OPPOSITE" SUPERVILLAIN

Sometimes a supervillain is the exact *opposite* of a superhero. Take the criminal who once fought against the Flash: **Turtle Man!** Because Turtle Man moved so slowly, the Flash just couldn't turn or stop in time to stop him. The superhero would just go flying by.

BIZARRO WORLD! After Lex Luthor shot a "duplicating ray" at Superman, it made an "opposite" copy of the Man of Steel—**Bizarro Superman!** Bizarro does everything in reverse, and lives on a cube-shaped planet called Htrae. (Spell it backwards!) People there are complimented for being ugly. Children are rewarded for being bad. And if you want to say "hello," you say "goodbye"!

THE SUPERHERO SUPERVILLAIN

If a villain has superpowers and wears a costume, then what's the difference between him and a superhero? Not much! In fact, lots of superheroes got their starts as supervillains. Think of the **Sub-Mariner, Rogue,** the **Black Widow, Hawkeye,** and **Mystique.**

But one supervillain is so awesome, he's less like a superhero and more like a god. He is **Galactus,** a being with powers so mighty no one knows their limits! By the time he got to Earth, Galactus had already destroyed hundreds of worlds once inhabited by billions of intelligent aliens.

And when Galactus showed up, he had a good speech prepared: "This planet shall sustain me until it has been drained of all elemental life. So speaks Galactus!"

Wow. That's the kind of line that you should use as much as possible.

Kid Holding Burrito: This burrito will sustain me until it has been drained of all elemental life. So speaks the Burrito Kid!

MY FAVORITE VILLAIN

The Fantastic Four have fought many superhero supervillains. But their archenemy is Victor von Doom (a.k.a. **Doctor Doom**). The parents of this evil genius were the dreaded Werner von Doom and a woman named . . . *Cynthia.*

Humph.

At college, young Victor von Doom majored in "demonic studies" and "superscience." And for his student project, he built a machine to contact dead people. Bad move! This machine exploded in von Doom's face and left him with lots and lots of hideous scars.

On top of that, von Doom got expelled from school, because using devices that talk with the dead were against the rules. (This is probably in your school handbook, too.)

So even though he didn't graduate from college, Victor called himself Doctor Doom. He started wearing a metal mask and suit. Then he set up shop in a castle named Doomstadt and got down to business. *Evil* business!

KNOW YOUR SUPERVILLAIN MOTTO!

1. The Riddler   a. "I'll get you next time, Gadget . . . next time!"

2. The Twiddler   b. "Kneel before Zod!"

3. Dr. Claw   c. "Twiddle me this . . ."

4. General Zod   d. "I hunger!"

5. Galactus   e. "Riddle me this . . ."

(See answers below.*)

* Answers: 1. e; 2. c; 3. a; 4. b; 5. d.

DIABOLICAL DIALOGUE!

Supervillains just can't shut up. It's their Achilles' heel! This weakness for talking is called "monologuing." (A *monologue* is a long speech by one person.) As noted in *The Incredibles*, evil geniuses love capturing superheroes and then explaining in great detail the hero's lameness and the villain's brilliance.

Luckily, this provides the superhero with one last chance to escape. But it also means that villains get to say the best lines—and here's the proof!

"Trust and affection—emotions I find alien and repulsive."—*Nekra*

"I *do* know the difference between right and wrong. Whatever the Scorpion does is *right*!"—*The Scorpion*

"You should thank me for killing you in so spectacular a setting."—*The Awesome Bravo*

"Why are those children leaning on wooden sticks?"—*Queen Atomia (After being told they're kids on crutches, Atomia says, "Bah! Why bother with weak people?")*

"You can't take it with you—so *I'm* takin' it with *me*!" —*Death-Man*

"I want exactly $49 million . . . and don't give it to me all in pennies!"—*Sinistro, Boy Fiend*

"We brought you back to life . . . just so we could kill you again!"—*Baron Von Evilstein*

"I've never killed superheroes before. It should be fun!" —*Manslaughter*

"Mirror, mirror, on the wall—who's the smartest crook of all? Me!"—*Mirror-Man*

"This man they call Batman . . . must be done away with. Perhaps we can contact him through the personal notice column in the daily newspaper."—*Dr. Karl Hellfern (a.k.a. "Doctor Death")*

"Emus bina dopta trysili stuntlitha."—*Mumbles**

"I *love* mass destruction! I bet I could be the best mass destructionist in the world."—*The Walrus*

"Farewell! You die as you lived—an *idiot!*"—*Hell-Blazer*

"You have stood in the way of art. I shall kill you for that." —*Daddy Longlegs*

"If you're going to conquer a whole planet, you might as well start someplace with a nice climate!"—*The Space Bunny*

"Kill! Kill! Kill! No . . . don't kill me! Not *me!*"—*The Mask*

"Fee fie foe fum! Bite off your heads, one by one!" —*Leviathan*

"I can restore the dead to life—I hope. But first I must kill you."—*Doctor Death*

"I abhor violence. Before I smother you to death with my enfolding clutch, I want you to know this truly grieves me." —*Elasto*

"Resistance is futile, maggot-scum."—*Firebolt*

"Since the instant of my birth, I have not taken a cleansing bath. Indeed, I've chemically *increased* my body odor . . . to *slay.*"—*The Skunk*

* Translation: "He must have been a dope to try a silly stunt like that."

THE SUPERVILLAIN HALLS OF SHAME AND FAME!

You almost have to admire some supervillains. After all, they can be pretty creative! Take the **Prankster.** He managed to get the legal rights to the entire alphabet. Yes, the Prankster owned the copyright to all twenty-six letters, from *A* to *Z*.

That meant that anytime someone wrote something in books, newspapers, or magazines, the Prankster got money from it. For example, Clark Kent's newspaper, the *Daily Planet,* had to pay the Prankster $2,000 a week!

But for every clever criminal like the Prankster, there's a very silly one that can make you wince.

THE FIVE LAMEST SUPERVILLAINS!

5. Hey, guess what **Polka-Dot Man**'s costume was covered with? Yep, dots. And with "advanced technology," Polka-Dot Man could use them as weapons. So small dots could be thrown like Frisbees. And Polka-Dot Man could use his big dots as flying saucers.

4. Lisa Snart was just a professional figure skater until she turned to *evil.* Then she was known as the feared **Golden Glider.** What was her superpower? She was able to figure skate—on *air.*

3. The Thing once battled a villain who wore "atomic boots." These shoes gave the bad guy the power to kick holes in buildings. The supervillain's name? **Goody Two-Shoes!**

2. **Kite-Man** (real identity: Charles Brown) flies around in a big kite. (Okay, it's a jet-powered hang glider, but still . . .) And then Kite-Man "shoots" deadly kites at people by blowing air behind them.

   Kite Man (singing): Let's go fly a kite . . . up to the highest height . . . and then destroy . . . *the world!*

1. Batman had to deal with a criminal named **Johnny Karaoke.** He was an assassin who liked to sing karaoke.

(Duh!) And as he sang, Johnny would pull a sword out of his microphone and kill his victim.

(Hey, I wonder what he'd do for an encore?)

THE BEST SUPERVILLAIN NAME EVER!

About fifty thousand years ago, a meteor crashed to earth. Nearby, a primitive caveman slept. Bathed in the meteor's radiation, this caveman became immortal––and really smart!

After waking up, the primitive man realized he had all of eternity to goof around. So he did two things.

- He changed his name to **Vandal Savage.** (Yes!)
- He decided to take over the world. (Hey, everyone needs a hobby.)

Over the years, Vandal Savage battled superheroes like the Flash and Green Lantern. But here's what I never got: since Vandal Savage was immortal, why didn't he just wait for the superheroes to *die?*

THE FIVE BEST SUPERVILLAINS!

5. The **Toyman** wore a green bow tie. But that wasn't his greatest crime! He was also an inventor who came up with *lots* of toy-based weapons, including:

   - A hand buzzer with a poisoned needle in the center
   - Exploding dolls
   - A giant jack-in-the-box that would boost him up walls
   - A flying pogo stick

   Amazingly, none of these ever stopped Superman.

4. **Gorilla Grodd** is an evil genius who controls humans using mental telepathy. Plus, he's a super-gorilla. How awesome is that? Grodd also gets a bonus score for appearing in stories like "In Grodd We Trust" and "The Apes of Wrath."

3. **Killer Moth** is a foe of Batman's. This villain drives a car called the Mothmobile. He wears a helmet with antennae. His sidekicks are named Larva and Pupa. And when Killer Moth is at home in his Moth Mansion, he sits on a throne of melted wax!

2. Ichabod Charles Earl Cream was known by his classmates as I.C.E. Cream. And he *hated* that nickname! So in science class, Ichabod became the **Ice Cream Hater.** His mission: to destroy all the ice cream in the world. It wasn't until a superhero persuaded the Ice Cream Hater to *try* some ice cream that his reign of terror ended.

1. The supervillain named **Badman** is unusual because he has a secret identity: Bruce Pain. (Get it?) Badman drives the Badmobile, which he parks in the Badcave. And his sidekick is named *Robber.* (Get it? Get it?)

SUPER SIDEKICKS!

Sidekick: An assistant with less authority than his or her boss.

Like many superheroes, you might think, "Sidekicks? Meh. Who needs 'em?"

You do! It's not so much that you need any help fighting crime. But even superheroes get lonely. It's a solitary life, washing your costume by yourself and keeping your secret identity a secret. Look, we all need someone to talk to. And it's even better if it's someone who won't talk back *and* can do the laundry!

Sidekicks are also useful for *public relations.* As a superhero, it's important that people like you. And a sidekick gives you someone that little kids can relate to. There's just something about a sidekick that people love!

Here's what I mean. Sure, **Sherlock Holmes** is a genius. But normal people can't relate to him. But pair off Holmes with the more ordinary **Dr. Watson,** and you've got a winner! And when Batman got started, he had a scary reputation as a "dark avenger." Yet after getting Robin as a sidekick, Batman became a kindly father figure. Batman and Robin were just two buddies having fun and fighting crime. Yay!

FOUR THINGS TO CONSIDER IN YOUR SIDEKICK

1. **Trustworthiness:** You want someone honest! Nothing is worse than a thieving sidekick who *side*swipes things. (Pun!) Obedience is also important. Your sidekick needs to understand you're not on a superpower trip. It's just that he's your second banana.

   And be sure your sidekick can keep a secret!

   You: And remember this above all: Don't tell anybody my secret identity.

   Sidekick: Oops—I just posted it on Facebook. Hey, five people already "Like" it!

   You: Yay! And also? You're fired.

2. **Age and Size:** To avoid looking silly, make certain to pick someone younger, shorter, and/or thinner than you.

3. **Clothing:** Never *ever* let your sidekick wear a cooler costume than yours.

4. **Superpowers:** You must be more powerful than your sidekick. So if you have *great* superpowers, your sidekick's powers can only be *good.* But if your superpowers are just *okay,* your sidekick's powers should be *weak.*

And it's perfectly fine if your sidekick has *no* superpowers at all. For example, Superman's sidekick is reporter **Jimmy Olsen.** And here's a list of Jimmy Olsen's superpowers:

- Red hair

- Freckles

- Annoying personality

Not very impressive, is it? Anyway, if you have an applicant who passes these standards, he still has to survive . . .

SUPERHERO ACTIVITY
THE SIDEKICK TEST

Supplies: Yoga mat or thick rug, someone who wants to be your sidekick.

Sidekicks don't need superpowers. But they do need to be good team players with some coordination. And they also need to be able to work with you while showing strength and courage!

1. Find a yoga mat or plush rug and lie on your back with your arms straight up.

2. Your wannabe sidekick takes off their shoes. Then they plant their feet on either side of your hips, facing *your* feet. Bending forward at the waist, they grab your ankles.

3. Now the tricky part! The sidekick needs to slowly raise one leg up and out. (It's sort of like a *side kick.*) As they do this, grab their ankle with the hand on that side of your body.

continued

Did your applicant pass the test? If so . . .

IT'S HIRIN' TIME!

The original **Robin** was a kid named Dick Grayson. His parents were high-wire performers until they were murdered. (Surprise!) But that Robin couldn't stay a boy wonder forever. After Dick Grayson grew up, the job of Robin went to a series of kids. One of these Robins was killed by the Joker, and another ended up getting murdered by his own clone. (Bummer!)

The lesson is that being a sidekick is dangerous. So before you make your new sidekick official, make sure that he or she completes and signs this form:

SIDEKICK ACCIDENTAL INJURY/DEATH WAIVER

I, [*your name here*], have volunteered for the job of "Superhero Sidekick." I realize that this will expose me to hazards such as falling out of buildings, being punched by supervillains, getting shot at with lasers, and wearing really tight underwear.

I will not hold my superhero responsible for any injuries I get in the course of my sidekick duties. Furthermore, if I die, I will not whine about it. Finally, I do not have any allergies to spandex that I am aware of.

Sidekick Signature: _______________________________

WITH NO POWER COMES *LOTS* OF RESPONSIBILITY

Congratulations on your new sidekick! Just think of him or her as a superintern. That means all of your chores now belong to your sidekick. And you don't even have to pay them! Here's just a few of the things your sidekick should be in charge of:

- Doing the laundry
- Managing your Twitter account

- Testifying in court
- Vacuuming the Secret Lair

*SIDE*NOTE

Since sidekicks get stuck with lousy costumes and lots of chores, the least you can do is give yours a good name. Sadly, most superheroes don't even do this much. For example, the original Human Torch had a sidekick named the **Flaming Kid.** That's not bad, but I think he should've been called Side-Burn!

EFFECTIVE MAN!   SIDE EFFECT!

Sadly, sidekick history is full of these naming tragedies. For example, the Flash had a sidekick named *Kid* Flash. But that's still better than the name that Amazing Man's sidekick got: **Tommy the Amazing Kid.** Zzzzzz.

The list goes on! Hydroman's sidekick was **Rainbow Boy.** The **Star-Spangled**

Kid was a superhero whose sidekick was **Stripesy.** And **Cat-Man** worked with an eleven-year-old girl named **Kitten.***

But my "Lame Name Award" goes to Daredevil. When this superhero first appeared, his sidekicks were four kids known as "the **Little Wise Guys.**" They were named Pee Wee, Jock, Scarecrow, and . . . Meatball!

SIDEKICK FAQs

Q. I've heard that superheroes always have to buy their sidekicks lunch. Is this true?

A. Yes. (You should also treat them to a breakfast muffin once in a while.)

Q. My sidekick wants her *own* sidekick. But is it even possible for me to have a *side*-sidekick?

A. Ha ha! That question is a real *side*splitter.

Q. What would happen if all the sidekicks got together and formed their own team?

A. This already happened! The **Teen Titans** included sidekicks like **Robin, Speedy, Wonder Girl, Kid Flash,** and **Aqualad.**

Q. Should I train a backup sidekick in case my regular one gets ill?

A. Yes. In superhero circles, this substitute is known as a "side-sick."

Q. My sidekick wants a promotion. How do I deal with this?

A. This is the biggest drawback for a sidekick—being stuck in a

* Cat-Man stopped fighting crime after he found a "claws" in his superhero contract.

dead-end job! The only way a sidekick can get promoted is if *you* die or retire. (See the problem?)

Q. Won't supervillains try to kidnap my sidekick to hold as a hostage?

A. Yes. That's why you shouldn't get emotionally attached to your sidekick. You may have to hire another one!

Q. Being a sidekick sounds pretty hard. How do I get anyone to take the job?

A. Are you kidding? Sidekicks lead a life of fame and glamor! Batman's creator, Bob Kane, said, "Every kid would like to be Robin . . . a laughing daredevil, free, no school, no homework, living in a mansion above the Batcave, riding in the Batmobile. It appealed to the imagination of every kid in the world."*

* Hey, what if Jessica Biel had a son and named him "Batmo"? (Think about it!)

Anyway, it's true that sidekicks have lots of chores. But they also have *way* less responsibility than superheroes.

Q. Who's *your* favorite sidekick?

A. My choice is a sweet little old woman named **Auntie May.** As Peter Parker's aunt, she somehow became Spider-Man's sidekick. This is weird because Auntie May was *really* old and *really* unhealthy. For more than thirty years she always seemed to be in a hospital bed or a wheelchair. So Auntie May's superpower was the ability to stand at death's door without actually going in.

But Auntie May had her adventures. For example, there was that time she needed a blood transfusion. So her nephew donated his blood. Bad move! His beloved Auntie Mae got radiation poisoning from Spider-Man's blood cells.

I *told* you she was always sick. Anyway, enough of this sidekick lore. It's time to play . . .

SUPERHERO ACTIVITY
SIDEKICK MANIA!

Supplies: Eight or more people, a
big area to run around in.

1. Choose one person to be the *sidekick* and one person to be the *superhero*. All the other players should pair off and link arms. (If you have an odd number of people, have one group of *three* people linking arms.)

2. The game starts with the superhero and the sidekick on opposite sides of the people in pairs. The sidekick wants to tag the superhero—and the superhero wants to avoid being tagged!

3. When the sidekick is ready, she says, "Shazam!" or some other cool word. And the race is on! To avoid being caught, the superhero can run to a pair of players and link arms with one of them. When he does, the player on the *other* side of the pair is the *new* superhero! Now he must run away from the sidekick.

4. If the sidekick successfully tags a superhero, then they reverse roles. (Or the successful sidekick can choose to trade places with any other player.)

ANIMAL SUPERHEROES!

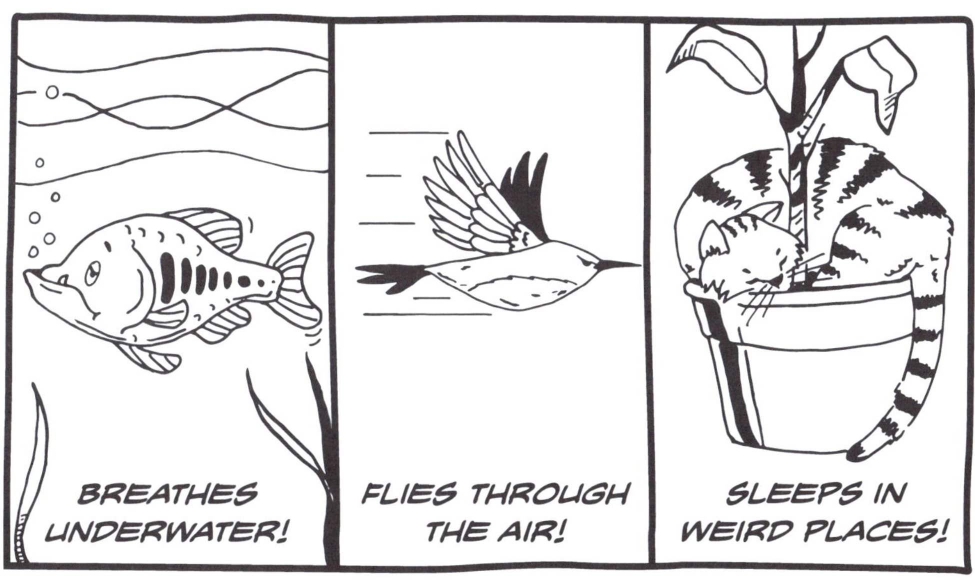

ANIMAL SUPERPOWERS

Let's face it, human sidekicks can be a total hassle. Instead of training, they're uploading selfies to their Web sites and showing off to their friends. (This explains why Spider-Man ditched his sidekick, **Alpha,** so quickly!)

And maybe that's why Superman has hung out with so many fine, furry friends! Below are some of them. See if you can spot the one I made up.

Streaky the Super-Cat

Krypto the Super-Dog

Beppo the Super-Monkey

Comet the Super-Horse

Hamish the Super-Hamster

Did you see through that question with X-ray vision? (Check out the answer below.*)

In the "real" world, lots of animals already have superpowers. For instance, did you know a naked mole rat can chew through concrete? And then there's a dog's supersmelling, a cheetah's lightning speed, and a chinchilla's ability to . . . chinch. Now, here are—

THE EIGHT GREATEST ANIMAL SUPERPOWERS!

1. **Invulnerability!** One animal just can't be destroyed. It's the **water bear** (a.k.a. "moss piglet"). This small invertebrate is found from the deepest oceans to the highest mountains. Water bears are at the North Pole and the equator. They can survive in hot springs at 300°F, or in the iciness of absolute zero.

   Water bears can survive ten years without water. They can survive being in outer space without a spacesuit. Oh, and they can survive 1,000 times more radiation than most animals—including humans.

   The water bear is indestructible! (And amazingly, it's sort of cute, too.)

2. **Superpunch!** Nothing on Earth comes close to punching as hard or fast as the **peacock mantis shrimp.** This

* Yes, the fake sidekick is Hamish the Super-Hamster.

colorful little animal has arms like hammers! And when the peacock mantis shrimp sees something it doesn't like, it *punches* it.

The shrimp developed its underwater punching ability to break the hard shells of mollusks, its main food. First, the shrimp's arm rockets forward almost as fast as a speeding bullet! At that speed, a bubble of air forms around the arm. When the blow lands, the bubble collapses and creates a powerful shock wave. And this shock wave is so strong, the peacock mantis shrimp can break out of an aquarium!

3. **Superstrength!** The *strongest* animal can easily pull well over 1,000 times its own body weight. If *you* were that strong, you could pull six school buses at once. So

is the strongest animal an ox? An elephant? A really buff Chihuahua?

No. It's the **dung beetle**! As you may know, dung beetles are beetles. Beetles that like to eat dung.

"What's dung?" you ask? Well, let's put it this way:

$$\text{DUNG} = \text{POOP}$$

So the world's superstrongest animal eats . . . *poop.* This might make you think that eating poop will give *you* superstrength. (If so, good luck with that!)

4. **Shape-Shifting!** The amazing **Indonesian mimic octopus** can change color more quickly than a chameleon. And it can also change its shape *and* behavior.

   So this octopus can undulate on the ocean floor like a flounder. Or it might spread its tentacles to look like the spiny (and venomous) lionfish. The Indonesian mimic octopus's best trick might be sneaking into a hole, where it makes one of it's tentacles striped. Then the octopus sticks the striped tentacle back *out* of the hole. And fish swim away in fear, because that tentacle looks like a poisonous sea snake!

5. **Regeneration!** If you lost your arm in a superhero accident, all you'd have left is a stump. Bummer! But if you had the superpowers of a newt, you could just grow a whole new arm back. And the arm would have complete muscles, nerves, bones, and skin. Amazing!

   The regeneration superstar in this category is the **axolotl.** It's a Mexican salamander that can regrow its tails, legs, and even parts of its heart, spinal cord, and *brain.*

6. **Superclimbing!** Spider-Man got his wall-crawling skills from a radioactive spider. But the best wall-crawler in the

animal kingdom is the little lizard known as the **gecko.** The gecko's feet are covered in tiny hair-like structures. These hairs act almost like one-way Velcro—anything they touch, they *stick* to!

As a result, a gecko can climb almost anywhere—including upside down on polished glass. In fact, a gecko can even hang its whole body weight from just *one* toe on a wall! (Let's see Spider-Man do *that.*)

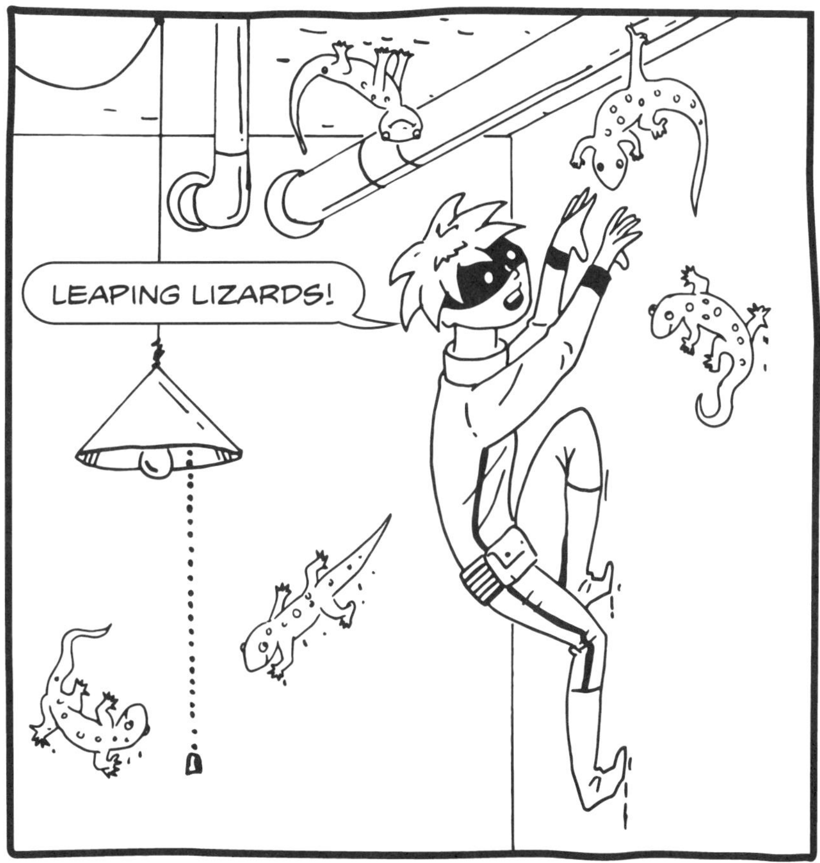

7. **Iron Armor!** At the bottom of the Indian Ocean, there's a big mollusk named the **scaly-foot gastropod.** It's unique because most shellfish have shells made of calcium. But

the outer layer of the scaly-foot gastropod's shell is made from *iron.* This makes the iron-armored mollusk safe from attacks by fish—and even most humans!

8. **Electrical Power!** There's a type of **knifefish** with some very special organs in its body. Each of these organs holds thousands of cells that can generate electrical "sparks." And if the knifefish combines all those cells together, it can make 600 volts of electricity. That's enough to kill a human!

   And that's how this knifefish got its nickname—the "electric eel."

Of course, there are more superanimals, but you get the idea.

Most of our superheroes use powers inspired by the animal kingdom! And sometimes superheroes even get their powers directly *from* animals. For example, the superhero called the **Black Condor.** See, as a young boy, he was raised by supersmart giant condors in Mongolia. By watching the huge birds, the Black Condor learned to fly himself.

Hmmm. Now that I think about it, that seems a little unrealistic.

Some superheroes even have animal parts. Take **Speed Centaur.** He has the upper body of a man and the lower body of a horse. ("Look at how fast that superhero gallops!") It would have been weird if Speed Centaur's *top* half was a horse. ("Look at how fast that superhero eats apples!")

MARVEL TAILS was a comic book with animals taking the place of famous superheroes. So after a pig named Peter Porker got superpowers, he became **Spider-Ham.** Other heroes included **Captain Americat,** the **Fantastic Fur,** the **X-Bugs,** and **Goose Rider.**

THE GREATEST ANIMAL SUPERHEROES

There are so many animal superheroes, where should I start? With **Atomic Bunny,** of course. After eating his radioactive Carrot Cubes, Atomic Bunny gets superstrength—*and* he can use his rabbit ears like hands!

Batman and Robin also worked with a great animal superhero. It started when the Dynamic Duo pulled a drowning dog from a river. Batman decided it could be helpful in collaring criminals. So the dog got a mask and a new name: **Ace the Bat-Hound.**

You may be wondering why a dog needed to wear a mask to keep his identity a secret. I can answer that in one word: *cats.*

As for Superman, he had a pet named **Krypto the Super-Dog.** (And Lex Luthor even had his own hound, named **Destructo.**) Krypto went on to lead the SCPA. You know, the **Space Canine Patrol Agents**? They were a group of superhero dogs with amazing powers.

See if you can match up the superhero dog with its abilities! (See answers below.*)

1. Tusky Husky	a. Used his tail like a lariat
2. Tail Terrier	b. Can turn into any animal you'd like
3. Bull Dog	c. Can tell the future
4. Prophetic Pup	d. Could grow a long tusk
5. Hot Dog	e. This dog could grow horns
6. Paw Pooch	f. Grows legs
7. Chameleon Collie	g. Gets hot

Does this seem goofy to you? Please! The SCPA fought many important battles against evil gangs like the **Cat Crime Club.** Oh, and I almost forgot! The SCPA had a battle cry that went like this:

"Big dog! Big dog! Bow wow wow!"

Okay, maybe that's a *little* goofy.

SECRET LAIRS!

Where do you work on your top secret superhero activities like [*deleted*], [*censored*], or [*redacted*]? That's right, your Secret Lair. What? You don't *have* a hidden headquarters? Then now's the time to get one.

Location is very important when setting up your Secret Lair. For starters, it should be in a spot where your parents can't find you. That means the best places are hidden caves, castles, abandoned warehouses, or active volcanoes.

Pop Quiz
GEOGRAPHY!

The address of the Xavier Institute for Higher Learning is . . .

a. 8149 Germone Road, Sebastopol, California

b. fictional

c. 1407 Graymalkin Lane, Salem Center, New York

So which is the right answer? Sorry, I'm not authorized to tell you that.

But in a pinch, tree houses or even your own bedroom can also work. Of course, if you're in your own room, evildoers like your sister will know where you are. So make up for this by making your Secret Lair superawesome!

SIX WAYS TO CUSTOMIZE YOUR SECRET LAIR

1. **Make It Sound Good:** Never again call it your "bedroom." Please! From now on, this is your Inner Sanctum, your Danger Room, your Secret Headquarters, or your Fortress of Solitude.

SECRET LAIR HALL OF FAME: Lex Luthor calls his secret hideout the **Nefarium.** That's where he keeps statues of his heroes, like Attila the Hun, Genghis Khan, and Al Capone.

2. **Decoration:** Your Secret Lair should reflect your own personality. So maybe you'll set up a trophy case. Or you might activate a giant hologram of yourself looking superhero-ey.

Ooh, and here's a great way to add some action to your walls—

Secret Lair Activity

SHADOW CATCHER!

Supplies: Glow-in-the-dark paint,
portable lights, brushes/rollers, colored
pencils or markers (like Sharpies).

Shadow-catching is a superpower that'll make your Secret
Lair kick. Here's how to do it:

1. Paint a wall of your room with glow-in-the-dark paint.

2. After the paint dries, bring in some portable
    lights, like floor lamps. Then get in a fighting or
    flying pose and stand next to the wall.

3. **Equipment:** Be sure to stock up on superhero supplies. And keep them within easy reach!

4. **Hiding Places:** You need good hiding places to stash your secret [*deleted*]. So choose these spots wisely!

HIDING SPOTS!

Of course, the *best* hiding place for your stuff is on another planet or in a different dimension. (Write to me for instructions on how to access these resources.)

5. **Defense:** Your enemies may get into your Secret Lair someday. By putting a fort or "safe room" inside it, you'll have a safe place to hide.

    Your bed, chairs, or dresser can all be used in your fort's construction. Building below or on top of tables is always fun. And good props include big pillows, sheets, blankets, cardboard boxes, and even giant blocks.

SIDEKICK'S FORT

MINI-SUPERHERO
SAFE ROOM

6. **Sidekick Trouble:** If your trusty companion doesn't like the nice fort you made, try using a kennel or large dog crate.

Two more small details. First, I recommend reinforcing the walls of your Secret Lair with five feet of steel-reinforced concrete. (Don't worry, your parents will understand.) Oh, and make sure to build a landing pad for your jet.

Whew! That was a lot of work. After spending all that time getting your Secret Lair just right, you need to get away from it. Seriously, you need a breath of fresh air! So head out and . . .

SUPERPOWER ACTIVITY
GAZE INTO INFINITY!

Supplies: Stars.

Sleeping outside under a starry sky is an important step in your superhero education. That's because gazing off into infinity allows you to think big superhero thoughts.

   Sleeping outside will improve your chances of contacting aliens from another world. Plus, if you're really lucky, you might see a meteor shower!

   It's also possible that your city may sponsor nighttime campouts. But however you go about it, unlocking the mysteries of the universe is a great way to unwind at the end of the day.

Optional: Get up early and watch the sun rise. (Of course, you'll need all of your superpowers just to get out of your sleeping bag.)

I guess it's time to end this chapter on Secret Lairs. But I have the strange feeling that I'm forgetting something important . . .

THE FIVE COOLEST SECRET LAIRS!

5. **The Batcave:** It's big, it's dark, and it has room for a giant crime laboratory. On the downside, dampness can be a problem.

4. **The Justice League Satellite:** This is where the **Justice League of America** hangs. Of course, it *is* orbiting the planet, which makes it a little hard to get to.

3. **The X-Mansion:** Not only do you get your own private room here, you can also work out in the Danger Room!

2. **The Fortress of Solitude:** Do you know what's cool about Superman's arctic hideout? It's a *fortress.* Plus, you can get some good solitude there.

1. **Latveria:** Doctor Doom uses an entire *country* as his hideout. Beat that, punks!

   The nation of Latveria at a glance:

GOVERNMENT:	Doctor Doom's dictatorship (duh!)
MAJOR HOLIDAY:	Doom's Day (celebrated anytime Doctor Doom says)
MAJOR AIRPORT:	Doomsport
CAPITAL:	Doomstadt
MONEY:	Doom Dollars*

* Okay, I made that one up. (But you have to admit, Doom Dollars sound pretty cool!)

SUPERHERO TEAMS!

PICKING TEAMS!

Think of a famous married superhero couple. Go ahead, take your time. *drums fingers, twiddles thumbs*

It's not easy, is it? And I'll bet you either chose Mr. and Mrs. Incredible or Mr. Fantastic and the Invisible Woman from the Fantastic Four. Right? Okay, now think of a famous superhero family with *kids.*

drums thumbs, twiddles fingers

You thought of the Incredibles again, right? Besides them, there really *aren't* that many superhero families. That's because the average superhero is an **"only child."** But this isn't a bad thing. Some people think that kids with brothers and sisters are less motivated than only children. So being an only child gives you a head start on superhero-dom.

But hey, don't cry if you *do* have siblings. I mean, I have *eight* brothers and sisters, and look how super I turned out.

thinking

Actually, you know what? Go ahead and cry. (I am!)

wiping away tears

Whew. Okay, I feel better now. Anyway, most superheroes were *only* children who were also *lonely* children. After all, their parents were usually "missing."*

So most superheroes start off as orphan loners—and when they grow up, it's hard for them to get together and cooperate with each other. And *that's* why supersquads always run into the same problem: big egos!

Lobster Girl: Hey, want to join my superteam?

Rooster Man: No thanks.

Lobster Girl (steamed): Huh? Why not?

Rooster Man: It's just hard to work with others when you're as awesome as I am.

A superhero team is like an all-star squad. All the players are great, but their teamwork stinks. Look at the X-Men. Its members are all loners—and the most popular one might be Wolverine. And he's the worse team player of all!

That's why every superhero team needs a superhero coach.

* By which I mean "dead."

So, are you ready for the challenge of forming your own supersquad? If so, start with a team-building exercise, like this:

SUPERTEAM ACTIVITY

SUPER TALES!

Supplies: Paper, pens/pencils, some comic books that nobody in the group has read.

Needs: Three to four players--or more.

1. One person is picked to be the *superhero*. She makes a scoresheet with each of the other players' names on it and selects a comic book

continued

randomly. Each of the other players writes their name on their own piece of paper.

2. The superhero shows the group the comic book and lets them look at the cover.

3. Then the superhero opens the comic book and writes down the story's *first complete sentence.* (No sound effects like "Bam!" or whatever.) At the same time, the other players invent their own first sentences for the comic book, based only on their look at the cover, and write them down.

4. The superhero collects all the papers, shuffles them, and reads them aloud. It's important not to crack up while doing so. The other players try to decide which of the sentences actually came from the comic book.

5. If someone votes for a player's invented sentence, the writer gets a point. If a player votes for the *real* sentence, that player gets two points! After the first round, the role of superhero rotates to another player.

The only superhero team to have snack time was the **Daydreamers.** It included a bunch of superkids, plus **Howard the Duck.** Their adventures took place in a fairy-tale land called Nevernevernarniozbia!

Now let's look at three different superhero teams. You should try to make *your* team like one of them—but which one? For starters, let's go with the most famous superhero team ever . . .

THE X-MEN

Formed: 1963

Home Base: X-Mansion, Westchester County, NY

Leader: Prof. Charles Xavier (Professor X)

Members: There have been over one hundred fifty different X-Men over the years. The original lineup was:

- Professor X (Charles Xavier)
- The Beast
- Iceman
- Cyclops
- Angel
- Marvel Girl

Later members included:

- Storm
- Wolverine
- Colossus
- Nightcrawler
- Rogue
- Psylocke

People born with the mutant "X-gene" get superpowers when they hit puberty. (As if being a teenager wasn't bad enough!) And here's what makes the X-Men unique.

The X-Men are less of a team and more like a *family*. So Professor X is the parent, and he keeps track of all his kids. Mutants. Whatever.

This superteam always has gobs of mutants coming and going. So cliques form, alliances are made, and there are *arguments--lots* of arguments!

There have been many quarrels about who the best and worst X-Men members are. My vote for the worst is **X-Man.** Yep, his name was X-Man and he was a member of the X-Men. That's x-tremely lame!

Speaking of arguments, that brings us to the next team—

THE AVENGERS

Formed: 1963

Home Base: Avengers Mansion, New York, NY

Battle Cry: "Avengers Assemble!"

Original Members: Thor, Iron Man, Ant-Man, the Wasp, and the Hulk. (Captain America joined a little later, after he got thawed out from an iceberg.)

The Avengers are famous for their horrible teamwork problems. I've narrowed these problems down to two major stumbling blocks:

1. Laziness and Distrust. When the Avengers are presented with a problem, no one superhero feels the need to do all the work. ("Why do I have to fix the satellite? Can't the Hulk take care of it?")

2. Keeping Secrets and Bad Communication. Some Avengers are spies. Others *assume* that the other superheroes have information, even when they don't!"

To stop all their bickering, the Avengers came up with rules. *Lots* of rules! Together, these rules make up something called a "charter." So whenever the Avengers have a question about something, they check the charter. For example, let's say they're wondering if they should take on a new challenge:

"The Avengers [can act], providing that the threat in question is super-powered, extra-terrestrial, extra-dimensional, sub-terranean, sub-oceanic, or occult, and engaged in an invasion, infestation . . . piracy, enchantment or any flagrant violation of international law . . ."

That's as clear as mud! And that leads us to our third superhero squad—

THE JUSTICE LEAGUE OF AMERICA

Formed: 1960

Home Base: Justice League Satellite in Earth orbit

Spin-Offs: Justice League Europe, Justice League International, Justice League Task Force, Justice League Elite, Extreme Justice

Original Members: Aquaman, Batman, the Flash, Green Lantern, the Martian Manhunter, Superman, and Wonder Woman.

The Justice League of America was assembled to battle villains that no single hero—even Superman—could take on solo. So who was their first awesomely scary opponent? **Starro the Conqueror!**

Starro was a really big starfish from another planet. After he came to Earth, he started mutating *our* starfish to help him take over our world. And of course, only a team of our greatest superheroes could stop a . . . giant starfish?

Anyway, the JLA members rely on *teamwork*. So here's how these superheroes tackle a problem:

1. Brainstorm.

2. Split up into small groups of two to three heroes. These groups take on different parts of the threat.

3. Come back together. Members share their work.

4. Make a united stand against the foe.

JOKE LEAGUE OF AMERICA: During a JLA meeting, Batman and Aquaman had a big argument. Both superheroes were mad, and after the meeting, Batman tweeted and Aquaman responded:

Batman @DkKnight Aquaman is a wuss. #gillface	6m
Aquaman @SeaKing Batman is Bruce Wayne. #payback	4m

TEAM LEADERSHIP!

Who's going to be in charge of your team? This is a superimportant question. Here's the way leadership works in the three teams we're talking about:

THE X-MEN:	Strong, fair leadership under Professor X.
THE AVENGERS:	Weak leadership under Captain America. (It's not his fault, though. *You* try getting the Hulk and Iron Man to sit down and listen!)
THE JLA:	Democracy, with a different leader for each assignment.

So now we've covered how these groups work. But what about their team personalities? A guy named Grant Morrison described it this way: The X-Men are like a bunch of kids in school. The Avengers are like the school's football team. And the Justice League is like a pantheon of gods.

So which team's style can *you* relate to best? Remember, there's no wrong answer . . . as long as you pick the Justice League of America! It has the perfect balance of mind and muscle, spandex and capes.

But the main reason the JLA comes out on top is because of what a hero named the Shoveler* said: *"We struck down evil with the mighty sword of teamwork and the hammer of not bickering."* The exception was when the JLA competed as a team in the Olympics. Aquaman was their coach, and he yelled a *lot.* "Superman, you're losing . . . get with it!" "Snap out of it, Flash!" "Strike three? You're blind as a Batman!" (Okay, I made that last one up.)

* He's a member of the superhero team called the Mystery Men.

PICKING A NAME

Your next step in getting your superhero team started is to pick a name. Let me just make a few suggestions:

- **No X's or Mutants.** The X-Men's popularity led to *lots* of other teams made up of misunderstood mutant teenagers. These include **X-Factor, Excalibur,** and the **New Mutants.** Enough already!

- **Keep It Short and Snappy.** And avoid initials! For example, The Higher United Nations Defense Enforcement Reserves is known as **T.H.U.N.D.E.R. Agents** for short. And the Amalgamated Universal Network to Inhibit Evil is called **A.U.N.T.I.E.** (Yeesh!)

- **Simple Is Good.** I always thought the **Defenders** had a really cool name.

- **But Clever Is Better!** The Teenage Mutant Ninja Turtles have a funny name. And they also spawned the best rip-off name for a superhero team—the **Radioactive Adolescent Black Belt Hamsters.**

GETTING MEMBERS

Now you're ready to start signing up superheroes for your team! So please be fair about allowing people to join. That means a superhero's gender, species, and birthplace can't count against them.

But there is *one* thing that can.

FOUR PEOPLE YOU DON'T WANT ON YOUR SUPERTEAM

1. In the 1930s, there was a superhero named the **Angel.** His "superpower" was the ability to cast his shadow in the shape of an *angel.*

   That's it!

2. **Dazzler** was a mutant with a weird superpower. She was a pop star who could turn music into bursts of light that *dazzled* bad guys. (No, I'm not joking.) Dazzler would say stuff like, "Got to boogie these suckers out!" And her foes included villains like Doctor Sax.

   The Dazzler was such a bad idea that the cover of the last issue of her comic book read, "Because you demanded it—the last issue of the Dazzler!"

3. **Archie** is a teenager who goes to Riverdale High. He seems like a nice enough kid, but his superpowers are limited to:

   - Having red hair with a tic-tac-toe grid on the sides
   - Knowing someone named "Jughead"
   - Being the only person named Archie in a band named the *Archies*!

4. The character named Poison Ivy can release chemicals that make people fall hopelessly in love with her. Take it from me—that's not good for team spirit!

INITIATIONS!

Before letting someone join up, give the superhero a test they have to pass. This "initiation" will make it a *little* hard to join your team. That way your new members will value their membership. They will also feel more loyalty to the group.

Different groups have different initiations. In the NBA, rookies have to wear pink Hello Kitty backpacks for a whole year. But that's too easy! So you may want to have new members perform good deeds when nobody is watching.

Of course, if no one is watching, it's a little hard to know when the initiation is done!

Remember, an initiation isn't the same as "hazing." That's when new members have to pass dangerous or humiliating tests to join. Hazing is *always* uncool—so don't make your membership test too hard!

SUPER RULES!

If you decide you want a charter (like the Avengers), here are some rules you might want to include:

- Every member should have at least one superpower. If it appears an applicant doesn't *have* a superpower, think hard. Do they know that plaids and stripes shouldn't be worn together? Then they have the superpower of *good fashion sense.* (They can join!)

- New members have to bring doughnuts to their first meeting. (That includes maple bars!)

- A new team leader will be elected each month.

- Being a coward is grounds for being expelled from the team— *unless* cowardice is the hero's superpower.

- Members who get kicked off the team must undergo hypnotic brainwashing. That way, they'll forget all of the team's secrets. (Don't worry, this only causes a little bit of brain damage.)

Okay, now's the time to gather your team members together, because I have the ultimate challenge for you punks superheroes! I like to call it . . .

SUPERTEAM ACTIVITY
MISSION: IMPROBABLE!

Supplies: Masking tape, red yarn (optional).
(Oh, and a house!)

1. Before people arrive at the house, tape long pieces of red yarn at different spots and angles across a stairway or crowded room. (If you don't have any yarn, long strips of masking tape also work well.)

2. When your team arrives, tell them that these "laser lines" will destroy anyone who touches them!

3. Challenge your team members to work through the lasers without making any of them move.

4. If a teammate does make a laser line move, it's not the end of the world. After all, it's just a strip of yarn! So to make everyone take this seriously, if anyone hits a laser line, shoot them with an actual laser.

Advanced Version: Lay out the laser obstacle course with directions. In some places, the players must go *over* them, in other spots, they must duck *under*. (And in some areas, there is hot lava that must be avoided at all costs!)

Be sure to have at least one spot where teammates have to jump over the lines onto some cushions. Oh, and have one more place where the laser lines are so thick, the players will have to use teamwork to get through them together!

So, did that exercise join your squad together? Or did it end with the end of the team? Sadly, I've seen many superhero teams dissolve over the years. But better for a team to dissolve than for it to become one of . . .

THE FOUR CRUMMIEST SUPERTEAMS!

4. The **Inferior Five** was a team of very unimpressive superheroes. For instance, they got around in a used car called the Inferi-Car. But with members like Awkwardman and the Blimp, what do you expect?

3. Batman's enemy, **Ra's al Ghul,** is a member of the **League of Shadows.** And it's not a very nice group. As Ra's al Ghul says, "[we've] been a check against human corruption for thousands of years. We sacked Rome . . . burned London to the ground. . . . Every time a civilization reaches the peak of its decadence, we return to restore the balance."

2. Joining the team of misfits called the **Doom Patrol** is like signing a death warrant! As longtime member **Robotman** said, "*Do other superteams lose members like the Doom Patrol? No. Of course not. If they did, nobody would get into the 'hero' business.*"

1. The worst superteam ever was known as **Justice League Detroit.** One of its members was **Vibe,** a break-dancer who had "the power to vibrate things." Vibe also liked to break-dance on street corners while wearing baggy yellow parachute pants.

Wow. The only way I can get that bad taste out of my mouth is with . . .

MY THREE FAVORITE SUPERHERO TEAMS!

3. The **Legion of Super-Heroes** is a team of superkids from the far future. Its members include Brainiac 5 (he has a "twelfth-level brain"), Triplicate Girl (she can split into three bodies), and Chameleon Boy. (BTW, Chameleon Boy's father got Yorggian Fever. Try not to bring it up.)

2. The **Metal Men** are robots named after metals like gold, iron, and tin. Silly, you say? Not at all! These metals provide the perfect team balance. See, Gold is the valuable leader. And Iron provides the muscle. (I admit Tin is pretty useless, but at least you can recycle him!)

   The Metal Men fought villains like Aluminum, Calcium, and Sodium. Not to mention Silicone and Polyethylene! (Seriously.)

1. The biggest superhero team of all time was the **Legion of Superfluous Heroes.** This team is *so* big, it takes over a year to do a complete roll call. Just a few of its members include:

Colossal Bore	Mucus Man
Crustacean Kid	Obnoxious Boy
Euphemism Lad	Pyromaniac Pete
Fan Boy	Rambunctious Boy
Flatulent Lass	
Gangrene Girl	Repugnant Kid
Generic Lad	Ruthless Lass
Glutinous Girl	Skintight Kid
Halfwit Lad	Sniveling Lad
Irrational Girl	Superficial Lass
Juvenile Kid	Unavoidable Boy
Lady Laxative	Yelling Girl

THE END IS NEAR!

ey, I just read a story called "The Last Days of Superman!" In it, the Man of Steel has to write his final words.

So Superman thinks really hard about his last message. What does he want to say? Finally he makes a decision! Then Superman flies to the Moon and uses his heat vision to burn gigantic words into the lunar surface.

After the moon dust clears, everyone on Earth can read his inspiring message:

DO GOOD TO OTHERS AND
EVERY MAN CAN BE A SUPERMAN

Superman also signed his message "*Superman,*" which cracks me up. (What, we were going to think *Aquaman* did that?)

I have to admit, that was a pretty good message. But still, I'd change it to:

DO GOOD TO OTHERS AND
EVERY PERSON CAN BE A SUPERHERO

In many ways, everyone already *has* superpowers. We can all get almost any information we want with the click of a button. We can peer deep into space—or spy on our neighbor's backyard. And right now, preschoolers are flying across the planet while watching superhero movies. (You know, in jets?)

But just *having* superpowers isn't enough to make someone a superhero. To earn that title, you need to be a good *role model.* So help others whenever you get the chance. And when you're competing, be a good loser.

Ha! I'm just kidding. You'll almost never lose—but be humble anyway!*

Most importantly, a superhero has to try to make the world a better place. You can do that in big ways ("I stopped a killer asteroid!") and small ones ("I rode my bike to school!").

As Thor said, "*The fate of your planet rests not in the hands of gods. It rests in the hands of mortals.*"

* I also suggest going to the bathroom *before* putting on your superhero costume. (You'll thank me for this later!)

Good call, Thunder God. Now let's get out there and save the planet! Sure, it's a lot of responsibility. But don't worry! What could possibly go wrong?

SUPER POP QUIZ!

What—you didn't know you had to pass a test at the end of the book? So much for your X-ray vision, hotshot!

But don't worry. This is an open-book test—you have to have this book *open* to take it. And don't try looking *back* in the book for answers (or *forward* to page 285 for the answer key), or something really bad might happen!

For example, you could lose your place. (That's why I use a superpowered bookmark!) But don't worry, these questions are really easy. Just look at this sample:

> Can you choose the correct answer?
> **a.** Yes. ☺
> **b.** No. ☹

Er, you did choose **a,** right? If so, good job! Make yourself a jelly sandwich—for energy—and then come back here and score 100 percent! (If *not*, put this book down and move to another planet.)

> *1.* One superhero who didn't get a start in comic books is
>
> _______________________________________.

2. "When everyone's super, no one will be." —Syndrome, *The Incredibles*

Discussion Question: Do you agree with Syndrome? Make your answer super by explaining why or why not.

____

____

____.

3. What hero has more superpowers than anyone else?

____.

4. If you fell off a five-hundred-foot-tall skyscraper, would you cry? ___________________________________.

5. Something makes Aquaman different from every other superhero. What is it? _________________________.

6. Imagine your town were being attacked by giant, superintelligent hamsters with X-ray vision. What would be the best way to stop these fearsome beasts? _________________

____

____

____.

7. This superhero uses a flying technique that would actually work. Who is it? ______________________________

8. Let's say you could have the superpower of being invisible from your elbows to the tips of your fingers. Would you want it? Why or why not? _________________________

____

____

____.

9. Did you know birds don't pee? Instead, their poop and pee just sort of combine. Weird, huh? ___________________

____.

10. Why is the following joke funny? Explain.

Q. Where do superheroes go on Father's Day?

A. The cemetery.

____

____

____.

11. Complete these mottos *and* identify the superhero who says them:

a. "Faster than ___________________________."

____.

b. "The guilty will be___________________________."

____.

c. "Imperius _______________________________."

____.

d. "In brightest day_____________________________

____"

____.

12. **Discussion Question:** A man named Kurt Vonnegut wrote, "We are what we pretend to be, so we must be careful about what we pretend to be." What do you think he meant by that?

____

____

____.

13. This superhero surprised readers by shooting and killing a criminal in the very first issue of his own comic book.

a. Bulletman

b. Batman

c. The Flash

14. This is the most famous style of kung fu:________________

____.

15. What's one of the worst superhero names ever?

____.

16. The weird thing about the original Human Torch is that he . . .

   a. wasn't human at all.

   b. burned everything he touched.

   c. was easy to find in hide-and-seek. ("You're getting
   warmer, warmer—yikes! Does anyone know where the
   fire extinguisher is?")

17. Superheroes call it "Amateur Night." The rest of the nation
calls it ________________________________.

18. What were Superman's two biggest ethical violations?

   a. ________________________________.

   b. ________________________________.

19. Originally the Hulk wasn't green. He was ______________.

20. Comic writer Daniel Clowes wanted his teenaged character,
Andy, to get superpowers in an unusual way. So after Andy . . .

   a. skipped showering, he became superpopular.

   b. smoked a cigarette, he got superstrength.

   c. wore a turtleneck, he became invisible.

21. Juvenile Kid is a member of the biggest superhero team of all
time. What's it called? ______________________

____.

22. **Discussion Question:** Imagine your superpower were the
ability to drink fifty gallons of water at one time. As we know,
every superpower has its downside. What problems might
this one give you? ______________________

____

____.

23. **True or False:** This is the best book of its kind ever written.

____.

EARLY SUPERHERO HISTORY!

Can you imagine a world without superheroes? I can't! That's because superheroes are everywhere—online, in comic books, on TV—and there's always new superhero movies arriving. (Heck, there was a reboot of the Spider-Man movie franchise in 2012, just five years after *Spider-Man 3*.) But it wasn't always this way. In the early twentieth century, people didn't even know what a "superhero" was!

1917: The word *superhero* is first used to describe a person of great accomplishments.

1920s: Japan is home to the world's first regularly published comic books. These *manga* books became so popular, special comic book libraries started lending out copies of the latest issues.

1932: Two American teenagers, Jerry Siegel and Joe Shuster, create an illustrated science fiction story called "The Reign of the Superman." (In it, "the Superman" is a bald, evil villain.)

1934: Siegel and Shuster change the character of Superman into a "good guy." They also give him a secret identity and an alien home. This version of Superman was unlike any hero ever seen. In fact, the Man of Steel was *so* original, publishers reject the idea for the next four years!

1938: Superman finally becomes the world's first comic book superhero. A star is born! (Or drawn.) Superman is so popular, and so many new superheroes follow him, the period from about 1938 to 1945 is called the Golden Age of Comics. About 130 different superheroes show up in this time.

1939: Inspired by Superman's success, artist Bob Kane and writer Bill Finger invent Batman. But Batman doesn't *wait* for crimes to happen. Instead, the dark, mysterious figure prowls the city at night, looking for trouble. Batman's first appearance is in *Detective Comics* (DC Comics). Marvel Comics also introduces two superheroes: the Human Torch and the Sub-Mariner. (And this is the year the first supervillain appears—an evil genius known as the Ultra-Humanite.)

1940: Will Eisner debuts his superhero, the Spirit. Eisner went on to become one of the most respected superhero artists ever, but it wasn't easy. He was a starving artist when he got started. Eisner once said, "When someone asks me what got me into comics, I can think of only one word: malnutrition." (Other new heroes include Captain Marvel, Robin, Green Lantern, and Daredevil.)

1941: About 15 million comic books are selling every *month,* and almost all of them are superhero titles. Captain America and Wonder Woman hit the newsstands for the first time. Also new are Green Arrow, Aquaman, Plastic Man, and Starman.

1942: The word *superhero* appears on a comic book cover for the first time.

1945: With the dropping of two atom bombs in Japan, superheroes who are affected by radiation start to appear, like Atomic Man.

1946: After the end of World War II, superheroes begin losing their popularity.

1952: The popular TV show *The Adventures of Superman* begins.

1954: A man named Fredric Wertham claims that comics are evil and lead young readers into lives of crime. He has no actual evidence, but this leads to the institution of the Comics Code. It forced comic books to be more wholesome. For example, comics had to always show police officers, parents, and judges in a respectful way. The Comics Code also said that "good shall triumph over evil and the criminal punished for his misdeeds" in *every* story.

1956: The unveiling of Barry Allen as the new Flash starts the Silver Age of comics. This begins the slow process of superheroes being cool and relevant again.

1961: A superhero team named the Fantastic Four arrives. They are unique for being reluctant superheroes who argue with each other. The FF stories also have "continuity"—events in one issue carry over to the next one. This helps Marvel become the most important superhero universe.

1962: The Amazing Spider-Man is something *new.* That's because Peter Parker is an insecure, sarcastic teenager. Once he gets superpowers, the first thing Peter does is try to make money, saying, "I just look out for number one—that means—*me!*" Spider-Man goes on to become one of the three most popular superheroes ever. (Also introduced this year: the Incredible Hulk.)

1966: Marvel introduces its first black superhero, the Black Panther. And on TV, the *Batman* show begins a two-year run. It was very silly; sometimes the actors were laughing so hard, filming had to be stopped. The silliness paid off, because the show was so popular, it aired twice a week!

1975: The X-Men are relaunched, and go on to become the world's favorite mutants.

1978: *Superman: The Movie* comes out. This is the first big-budget superhero movie with decent special effects. (It won't be the last.)

1984: First appearance of the Teenage Mutant Ninja Turtles.

1986: Frank Miller's *Batman: The Dark Knight Returns* comes out, returning Batman to his scary roots. The same year, Alan Moore's *Watchmen* continues the trend of thoughtful superheroes in dark stories.

1992: A number of Marvel's most popular artists start a comic book company called Image. Its superhero titles include *Spawn, Youngblood,* and *WildC.A.T.S.*

1993: Superman dies (gasp!), killed by a creature called Doomsday. No worries, though. The Man of Steel came back a few months later with a mullet.

1995: Peter Parker's Aunt May *finally* dies (see page 229). She *doesn't* come back with a mullet.

2000s: Things sure get complicated! By now, superheroes like Spider-Man have been around so long they don't have a single story anymore. Their history is a tangled web! That's why many superheroes just start over in alternate universes. In 2011, DC takes all of its important superheroes and begins them again with a new issue #1.

SELECTED BIBLIOGRAPHY

Aiken, Katherine. "Superhero History: Using Comic Books to Teach U.S. History." *OAH Magazine of History* 24, no. 2 (April 2010): 41–47.

Allain, Rhett. "Is It Possible to Run Up a Wall? Sort of." *Wired.com: Dot Physics,* July 24, 2012. www.wired.com/wiredscience/2012/07/can-you-run-up-a-wall/.

Arbesman, Samuel. "What to do if your child has superpowers." *Boston Globe,* June 21, 2009. www.boston.com/bostonglobe/ideas/articles/2009/06/21/what_to_do_if_your_child_has_superpowers/.

Beatty, Scott. *The Batman Handbook: The Ultimate Training Manual.* Philadelphia: Quirk Books, 2005.

Benton, Mike. *Superhero Comics of the Golden Age: The Illustrated History.* Dallas: Taylor Publishing, 1992.

Coogan, Peter. *Superhero: The Secret Origin of a Genre.* Austin, TX: MonkeyBrain Books, 2006.

Cronin, Brian. *Why Does Batman Carry Shark Repellent?* New York: Plume, 2012.

Daily, James, and Ryan Davidson. *The Law of Superheroes.* New York: Gotham Books, 2012.

DeBenedet, Anthony T., and Lawrence J. Cohen. *The Art of Roughhousing: Good Old-Fashioned Horseplay and Why Every Kid Needs It.* Philadelphia: Quirk Books, 2010.

DiPaolo, Marc. *War, Politics and Superheroes: Ethics and Propaganda in Comics and Film.* Jefferson, NC: McFarland, 2011.

Doctor Metropolis [pseud.]. *How to Be a Superhero.* New York: Plume, 2004.

Duin, Steve, and Mike Richardson. *Comics: Between the Panels.* Milwaukie, OR: Dark Horse, 1998.

Edwardes, Dan. *The Parkour and Freerunning Handbook.* New York: HarperCollins/It Books, 2009.

Feiffer, Jules. *The Great Comic Book Heroes.* Seattle: Fantagraphics Books, 2003.

Glenn, Joshua, and Elizabeth Foy Larsen. *Unbored: The Essential Field Guide to Serious Fun.* New York: Bloomsbury, 2012.

Goulart, Ron. *Comic Book Encyclopedia.* New York: HarperCollins/It Books, 2004.

Gresh, Lois H., and Robert Weinberg. *The Science of Superheroes.* Hoboken, NJ: Wiley, 2002.

———. *The Science of Supervillains.* Hoboken, NJ: Wiley, 2005.

Hill, Kyle. "The God of Thunder, and Momentum." *Scientific American Blogs,* February 7, 2013. http://blogs.scientificamerican.com/guest-blog/2013/02/07/the-god-of-thunder-and-momentum/.

Horn, Maurice, ed. *The World Encyclopedia of Comics.* 2nd ed. Broomall, PA: Chelsea House, 1998.

Howe, Sean. *Marvel Comics: The Untold Story.* New York: HarperCollins, 2012.

Hughes, Jamie A. "'Who Watches the Watchmen?': Ideology and 'Real World' Superheroes." *The Journal of Popular Culture* 39, no. 4 (August 2006): 546–57.

Jay, Timothy, and Kristin Janschewitz. "The Science of Swearing." *Observer* 25, no. 5 (May/June 2012). www.psychologicalscience.org/index.php/publications/observer/2012/may-june-12/the-science-of-swearing.html.

Jones, Gerard, and Will Jacobs. *The Comic Book Heroes: The First History of Modern Comic Books from the Silver Age to the Present.* Rocklin, CA: Prima, 1996.

Kakalios, James. *The Physics of Superheroes.* 2nd ed. New York: Gotham Books, 2009.

Konnikova, Maria. *Mastermind: How to Think Like Sherlock Holmes.* New York: Viking, 2013.

Koren, Marina. "Virtual Superhuman Powers Translate into Real Life Helpfulness." *Smithsonian.com: Surprising Science,* January 31, 2013. http://blogs.smithsonianmag.com/science/2013/01/virtual-superhuman-powers-translate-into-real-life-helpfulness/.

Koster, Kevin. "Incredible HULK Provocations or 'Ways to make Dr. David Banner angry.'" http://kennethjohnson.us/HulkOutList.html.

Langley, Travis. "Why Do Supervillains Fascinate Us? A Psychological Perspective." *Wired.com: Underwire,* July 27, 2012. www.wired.com/underwire/2012/07/why-do-supervillains-fascinate-us/.

Morrison, Grant. *Supergods: What Masked Vigilantes, Miraculous Mutants, and a Sun God from Smallville Can Teach Us About Being Human.* New York: Spiegel & Grau, 2011.

Muir, John Kenneth. *The Encyclopedia of Superheroes on Film and Television.* 2nd ed. Jefferson, NC: McFarland, 2008.

Powell, Michael. *The Superhero Handbook.* New York: Sterling, 2005.

Rachael Rabbit [pseud.]. "Paper Roll Craft: Super Hero Bracelets." Rachael Rabbit: Handmade with Love. April 17, 2013. http://rachaelrabbit.blogspot.com/2013/04/toilet-roll-craft-super-hero-bracelets.html.

Reynolds, Richard. *Super Heroes: A Modern Mythology.* Jackson, MS: University Press of Mississippi, 1994.

Robbins, Trina. *The Great Women Superheroes.* Northampton, MA: Kitchen Sink, 1996.

Rosenberg, Robin S., with Jennifer Canzoneri, eds. *The Psychology of Superheroes: An Unauthorized Exploration.* Dallas: BenBella Books, 2008.

Rovin, Jeff. *The Encyclopedia of Superheroes.* New York: Facts on File, 1985.

———. *The Encyclopedia of Super Villains.* New York: Facts on File, 1987.

Shutt, Craig. *Baby Boomer Comics.* Iola, WI: Krause, 2003.

Sims, Chris. "Ask Chris" column. *Comics Alliance.* www.comicsalliance.com/category/ask-chris/.

Svetkey, Benjamin. "What About Wonder Woman?" *Entertainment Weekly,* November 26, 2010.

Telis, Gisela. "Mantis Shrimp Smash!" *ScienceNOW,* June 7, 2012. http://news.sciencemag.org/sciencenow/2012/06/mantis-shrimp-smash.html.

Thaler, Andrew David. "Five organisms with real super powers that rival their comic book counterparts." *Southern Fried Science,* January 2, 2013. www.southernfriedscience.com/?p=14057.

Tulley, Gever, and Julie Spiegler. *50 Dangerous Things (You Should Let Your Children Do).* New York: New American Library, 2009.

Weinstein, Simcha. *Up, Up, and Oy Vey! How Jewish History, Culture, and Values Shaped the Comic Book Superhero.* Baltimore: Leviathan, 2006.

Weldon, Glen. "They Call Me . . . Bruce? When Characters Outlive Their Names." *NPR: Monkey See,* February 1, 2013. www.npr.org/blogs/monkeysee/2013/02/01/170842610/they-call-me-bruce-when-characters-outlive-their-names.

Wilson, Daniel H. *Bro-Jitsu: The Martial Art of Sibling Smackdown.* New York: Bloomsbury Books, 2010.

Wolchover, Natalie, and Life's Little Mysteries [pseud.]. "Could a Penny Dropped Off a Skyscraper Actually Kill You?" *Scientific American Blogs,* March 5, 2012. www.scientificamerican.com/article.cfm?id=could-a-penny-dropped-off.

Wright, Bradford W. *Comic Book Nation: The Transformation of Youth Culture in America.* Baltimore: The Johns Hopkins University Press, 2001.

Yong, Ed. "Exposed: The severe ethical breaches of superhero journalists." *Discover: Not Exactly Rocket Science,* June 27, 2012. http://blogs.discovermagazine.com/notrocketscience/2012/06/27/severe-ethical-breaches-superhero-journalists/#.Ubn58I58tUM.

Zehr, E. Paul. *Becoming Batman: The Possibility of a Superhero.* Baltimore: The Johns Hopkins University Press, 2008.

———. *Inventing Iron Man: The Possibility of a Human Machine.* Baltimore: The Johns Hopkins University Press, 2011.

———. "Bumps and Bruises from Bruce to Batman, and Beyond." *Scientific American Blogs,* December 4, 2012. http://blogs.scientificamerican.com/guest-blog/2012/12/04/bumps-and-bruises-from-bruce-to-batman-and-beyond/.

Zielinski, Sarah. "The Top 10 Animal Superpowers." *Smithsonian.com,* December 6, 2012. www.smithsonianmag.com/science-nature/The-Top-10-Animal-Superpowers-182396261.html.

ANSWER KEY

1. The Green Hornet.

2. The only wrong answer is one you didn't explain! (Also, here's a Fun Fact: Syndrome was drawn to look like the director of *The Incredibles*, Brad Bird.)

3. J'onn J'onzz, the Martian Manhunter.

4. I'd hope not, because superheroes don't cry! (But they do die sometimes, though.)

5. He probably has a gas bladder.

6. One possibility would be to make huge exercise wheels and put them at the edge of town. No way those giant, superintelligent hamsters could resist taking them for a spin.

7. Thor!

8. I have no idea of what the right answer to this question would be. But I do know it would totally freak people out if you shook hands or fist-bumped them with your invisible hands!

9. Yes, it is weird. Imagine if humans were the same way—
now *that* would be a crazy superpower.

10. Well, many superheroes have fathers who are, um, sort
of . . . *dead.*

11. **a.** "Faster than . . . a speeding bullet." (Superman. BTW, is
there such a thing as a *slow* bullet?)
 b. "The guilty will be . . . punished." (the Punisher)
 c. "Imperius . . . Rex!" (Sub-Mariner)
 d. "In brightest day . . . in blackest night/No evil shall escape
my sight/Let those who worship evil's might/Beware
my power—Green Lantern's light!" (What? You haven't
memorized Green Lantern's motto yet?)

12. Did you give a thoughtful answer? (If not, just pretend
you did!)

13. **b.** Batman.

14. *Wing Chun!*

15. Good examples might include Minimidget, Adam X the
X-Treme, Pepper Potts, the Human Nightlight, and Qwyk'sand
Wyndzbane.

16. **a.** The original Human Torch wasn't human. He was an
android made by a scientist.

17. Halloween.

18. **a.** Being a reporter who reported on himself.
 b. Owing the government billions of dollars in taxes.

19. Pink—no, gray!

20. **b.** This doesn't work, you know!

21. The Legion of Superfluous Heroes.

22. For one thing, you'd have to go wee wee wee all the way home.

23. If this were any more true, it would hurt!

ACKNOWLEDGMENTS

I wrote this book all by myself. (Don't look so surprised! I am a superhero, y'know.)

However, my sidekicks *tried* to help. So many, many thanks to Melinda "Colonel Unstoppable" King, Eric "Dennis the Phantom Menace" Danko, Django "Vandal Samurai" Jacobsen Fein, Rudy "Radioactive Lad" Pinedo, Kristin "Ripcord" Schlupp, Mitchell "Death Stache" King, Michelle "@$#! Girl" Witte, Mike "Vowel Dude" Lkb, Angela "the Squire" Root, Greg "Electro-Guardian" Stearns, Janice "Mega-Gal" Johnson, Evan "Unavoidable Man" Kiester, Gretchen "Lobster Lady" Lancour, Bob "Kingpin" Kingston, Jill "JCLA" Corcoran, Donna "Dynamite Sight" Matias, Patricia "Queen Bee" Prince, Karen "Wicked Awesome Grrrl" Washington, Michael Ivan "the Phantom Radical" King, Katy "Dappled Lightning" Fackler, David Michael "Crater Hater" Slater, Benjamin "Punctuation Person" Herson, Judith "Fancy Pants Lass" Thompson, James "Margarine Man" Butterfield, Holden "Afro Warrior" Hindes, Lynn "Coffee Achiever" King, Bob "Baron Redoubtable" Cooper, and Suzanne "Super Scoop" Taylor.

And finally, thank *you*. Remember, even when the rest of the world is bizarro, you're still perfectly normal!